THE MEANING OF

THE IDYLLS OF THE KING

AN ESSAY IN INTERPRETATION

BY

CONDÉ BENOIST PALLEN, LL.D.

AUTHOR OF "THE PHILOSOPHY OF LITERATURE," "EPOCHS
OF LITERATURE," "THE FEAST OF THALARCHUS,"
"THE DEATH OF SIR LAUNCELOT," ETC.

HASKELL HOUSE

Publishers of Scholarly Books

NEW YORK

1965

published by

HASKELL HOUSE
Publishers of Scholarly Books
30 East 10th Street • New York, N. Y. 10003

Library of Congress Catalog Card Number: 65-26453   5

FOREWORD

THE letter of Lord Tennyson, the facsimile of which appears on the first page, was written in commendation of a brief magazine article on *The Idylls of the King* published in 1885. The interpretation of the article of 1885 was more fully developed in a series of short studies, also published in magazine form in 1895. The present essay is a still further amplification of the original conception, to which is added an appendix of notes elucidating some points passed over in the text. The author has thought it better to treat these points apart, in order to avoid unnecessary digressions from the main tenor of his theme. This study is now printed in book form, in response to repeated requests to put the interpretation in a more convenient shape than the pages of a magazine afford.

CONTENTS

Aldworth,
Haslemere,
Surrey.

Ap: 4th
— 85

Sir,

I Thank you for your critique
on the Idylls of the King. You see
further into their meaning than most
of my Commentators here done

Yours faithfully

Tennyson

Mr Conde B Pallen
New York City
U. S. A.

THE MEANING OF THE IDYLLS
OF THE KING

THE GENERAL PURPORT OF THE IDYLLS

WHY should any one set about the interpretation of the Idylls? Is not their meaning plain enough in itself—so many vignettes illustrating a common theme and tracing the Arthurian legend through some of its most touching episodes in the subtle imagery of Tennyson's polished muse? Mere idylls, summer landscapes of a tender fancy weaving the myths of an ancient fable into modern verse, graceful pictures of heroic days blown by the winds of tradition into this hurly-burly age of sturdy fact and despotic practicality? What need, then, of plunging into seas of allegory to find a mystic meaning beneath the glittering pageantry of the poet's lines? Take them for what they themselves appear to be, random pictures of an heroic legend, done by a master's hand, but withal

7

mere pictures, whose beauty and whose worth lie in the master's use of color, light and shade, to body forth the outward show, the pomp and the splendor of the Arthurian myth—this and nothing more.

Idle the office of interpretation if forestalled by such a prejudice. Yet such has been the current notion; a notion, it must be conceded, not lacking extenuation; for the Idylls were given to the world without regard to their proper order, a circumstance contributing not a little to the popular misunderstanding of their real scope and purpose. The last Idyll of the twelve was published first, framed in a poem entitled *The Epic*, in which the *Morte D'Arthur* was described as the fragment of a larger work. The remaining eleven came out at wide intervals without regard to the chronological or logical order of the theme of which each is a due integral part. The natural judgment was that the Idylls, though clustered about the Arthurian legend, had no closer bond than the hazard of the same heroic subject in such phases as struck a poetic fancy. It was not until after ten Idylls had found their way to the light that they were grouped together in their due relation.

Whether or not *The Idylls of the King* may

justly lay claim to the dignity and proportions of an epic poem, at least there is no gainsaying—by one who has read them in the order in which they are arranged in authorized editions subsequent to 1884—that they constitute a single poem with an intimate relation both as to time and theme.

But more than this, whether epic or not, they are a poem whose theme is deeper than the surface, not mere tableaux of wondrous coloring and pose, appealing only to the eye and the fancy. The placing of a further value on them than their mere outward show has indeed been disputed, and it has been averred that a deeper meaning has been *read into* them than they themselves will warrant to be read out. But such criticism seems to arise rather from the prejudice of a popular misconception than from any discriminating consideration of their intrinsic nature. More than this, we may urge that criticism of the kind, denying their esoteric meaning, impinges on an awkward predicament of its own making; for if the Idylls be mere poetic pageantry, they are not always even that, but in many respects a mere masquerade of airy imagery, beautiful but unsubstantial. Regarded from this external view only, it becomes necessary to explain satisfactorily innumerable obscure passages, which have no significance under this mere word-painting theory, as well as to give the chief characters and the main action of the drama a rational perspective. Who is Arthur, who, though wounded, cannot die; whose coming and whose passing are a mystery beyond the ken of men, since " from the great deep to the great deep he goes"? Who Merlin, the sage, and, above all, the Lady of the Lake, who dwells at the bases of the hills? Who the three Fair Queens, destined to help Arthur at his need? What is Excalibur, the mystic weapon given to Arthur by the Lady of the Lake at the installation of the Round Table, to be returned to her at his passing? What is the mystic city of Camelot, built to music, therefore never built at all, and therefore built forever? These and other aspects of the Idylls, utterly un-intelligible on the word-painting theory, it may be urged, are but the unwitting inheritance of the old legend, and Tennyson's heroics are only un-meaning echoes of the ancient mysticism. Yet the mystical element is there, and those who would deny its significance in the Idylls must bear upon their shoulders the onus of proof that the poet has not seized upon those legendary shadows of higher things to body forth his own conception of his ideal, molding them after the fashion of his own genius.

Apart from the inconsistency of this merely external view of the Idylls and the inexplicable riddles it leaves behind it at almost every page, we may urge the words of Tennyson himself, giving us more than a quickening hint as to the profounder sense of the poems. First as to their unity, the perception of which is primarily essential to their proper understanding: that unity will of course most conclusively stand forth from a consideration of their intrinsic character. But prior to such demonstration it finds extrinsic support from passages in the poem entitled *The Epic*. *The Epic* is but the poetic envelope of the *Morte D'Arthur*, which the poet calls a fragment of a larger work and which was the first Idyll published, though at the time in an incomplete state.

The point I would urge is that we may gather Tennyson's mind from certain lines in *The Epic*. Everard Hall, a poet, sits, on a Christmas eve, around the " wassail bowl " in company with boon friends. The subject of an epic poem Hall had written at college is brought up:

.   .   "You know," said Frank, "he burnt
His epic, his King Arthur, some twelve books,"

And then to me, demanding "Why?" "Oh, sir,
He thought that nothing new was said, or else
Something so said 'twas nothing—that a truth
Looks freshest in the fashion of the day.
God knows he has a mint of reasons: ask.
It pleased *me* well enough." "Nay, nay," said Hall
"Why take the style of those heroic times?
For nature brings not back the mastodon,
Nor we those times; and why should any man
Remodel models? These twelve books of mine
Were faint Homeric echoes, nothing worth,
Mere chaff and draff, much better burnt." "But I,"
Said Francis, "picked the eleventh from this hearth,
And have it. Keep a thing, its use will come.
I hoard it as a sugar-plum for Holmes."

.   .   .   .

.   .   . And the poet, little urged,
But with some prelude of disparagement,
Read, mouthing out his hollow o's and a's,
Deep-chested music, and to this result.

The passage is quoted at some length to put its
full purport before the reader. Everard Hall, the
poet, is clearly Tennyson himself. It may, with
some show of point, be urged that this is no evidence that Tennyson had actually written an epic,
that the fiction of an epic of twelve books was

simply a fanciful setting for the *Morte D'Arthur*.
Admitting the force of this, we have at least evidence of Tennyson's conception of the possibility
of an epic out of the materials of the Arthurian
legend; and if he had not actually executed it, we
at least understand that the purpose, and perhaps
the plan, was in his mind's eye. But what is especially notable in this passage is that it gives us a
clear expression of the character of the epic,
whether already written or merely contemplated.
This we gather readily from the line "that a truth
looks freshest in the fashion of the day." The
burnt epic the poet regarded as the vehicle of a
truth, better conveyed after a later fashion, better told in other ways than in heroics. Therefore
he had discarded the old setting of that truth,
deeming it more acceptable to modern ears in the
fashion of a day other than the style of those
heroic times. The epic, then, was not to be a mere
rehearsal of King Arthur's exploits, but, more than
this, the poetic setting of a great truth to be ut-
tered to the world. What that truth is we are
not told in this prelude to the *Morte D'Arthur*.
Sufficient to glean from its lines that there is in-
tended a truth about which the poet has used, as a
painter would his colors, the beauties of the old

legend to body forth an ideal too often forgotten
by a generation blinded by the pride of its own
philosophies.

Evidence we have here sufficient to show us that
the Idylls are more than mere vignettes of an ancient tale.   But further evidence we also have in
Tennyson's own words what that inner truth is.
In the epilogue to the Idylls is a passage which
puts the matter beyond all doubt.   Addressing the
Queen the poet says:

.   .   .   But thou, my Queen,
Not for itself, but thro' thy living love
For one * to whom I made it o'er his grave
Sacred, accept this old imperfect tale,
New-old, and shadowing Sense at war with Soul
Rather than that gray king whose name, a ghost,
Streams like a cloud, man-shaped, from mountain peak,
And cleaves to cairn and cromlech still: or him
Of Geoffrey's book, or him of Malleor's, one
Touched by the adulterous finger of a time
That hovered between war and wantonness,
And crownings and dethronements.

The keynote is here plainly enough sounded.
It is a tale *shadowing Sense at war with Soul,*

* The Prince Consort.

not simply the mythical story of a fabled king on the lips of popular tradition, nor of the knightly hero depicted in Geoffrey's or Malory's olden book![1] Sense at war with Soul is the esoteric character of *The Idylls of the King*, and this is that truth, new-old, which the poet, Everard Hall, thought better told in the fashion of the day, but which a maturer sense of the plastic power and poetic worth of the old legend led the poet to embody, after all, in the style of those heroic times. In face of this passage from the epilogue there can be no room for legitimate doubt as to the meaning of the Idylls. Without this interpretation put upon them they become in large part so many poetized riddles, valueless save for the subtleness and beauty of their imagery. In the light of this interpretation they become a luminous message of purity to an age

> Touched by the adulterous finger of a time
> That hovered between war and wantonness.

To Tennyson, in an age whose literature has become replete with the gross spirit of realism, we are indebted for a noble poem whose theme is the exaltation of the beauty of purity, and this, where

[1] The numbers refer to the notes on pages 105 to 115.

the age is most blind to it, in man. The message is luminous to those who have desire to see. By the deaf and blind unto holy things, the voice will not be heard, the light will not be seen, and

> . . . The crime of sense becomes
> The crime of malice, and is equal blame.

It is this crime of sense become the crime of malice which undoes the building up of Arthur's realm, breaks the harmony of the virtues into the discord of sin and crime, and disrupts the order Divine Wisdom has established amongst men. Against it the spiritual man, despite of the sin, the crime, and the treachery about him, stands proof, passing from the old order in the flesh to the new order in the spirit. The Idylls are simply the drama of the new-old truth, Sense at war with Soul, the old battle and the ever renewed strife between the old and the new man. The picture is old but its meaning ever new, speaking significantly to a generation sunk in the steaming valleys of sense, and blinded to the lofty ideal on the heights above by the gross exhalations of its materialism.

The poet puts the picture before us in an allegory. While to a proper understanding of the

Idylls we must realize the allegorical character of the poem speaking to us in symbols, we must not forget the artistic perspective which such a work demands. We must take the parts in their proper proportions. Like any other picture, it has its coloring, its lights and its shadows, massing effects here, softening its points there, with its foreground and its background, yet the whole breathing the same organic inspiration. We must not look for an allegory in every passage, a symbol in every line, a mystery in every syllable, a hidden meaning in every image. This were driving interpretation to the ridiculous, straining at a gnat to swallow a camel, and making art a mere artificial symbol. While detail and incidents serve the purpose of the main idea, illustrate and embellish the action and development of the argument, they are not to be taken for the essence of the movement nor emphasized to a microscopic magnitude.

The mechanism of art is not to be confounded with its ultimate aim or its ideal. Unfortunately, the ideal of art is often obscured by the crime of sense. The function of art is to express the splendor of truth, and modern man in large part has either denied outright or become skeptical of the truth. The ideal lost, he has been thrown back upon the mechanism of art. We have therefore much finished painting, wrought to an exquisite nicety of detail, but barren of the ideal; we have much elaborated versification, but little true poetry; much building, but little architecture; a vast deal of formal symbolism, but no true spirituality. There is neither inspiration nor aspiration where there is no ideal; no ideal where truth is neglected or denied. Truth is the root of art. Sapless and barren, therefore, the product of the art effort without it. We have much artifice, but little art.

The degeneration has not stopped here. Not only has the ideal been abandoned, but in the errant madness of the hour an idol has been erected in its stead, and we have the fetich worship of the ugly by the school of Naturalism. Here is the adoration of not even the golden calf, but of a beast of clay. Worse than mere artifice, it is the parody of art. The abode of its choice is with the swine, and it no longer sighs for the glory of the Father's house. The crime of sense has become the crime of malice. To depict man, not with the splendor or the glory of truth upon his brow, but man, the beast, amid the husks and the swine, has become an avowed intent and end. The ugly, the gloom of falsehood, not the beautiful, the splendor of truth, is its sodden idol. It is without ideal. Here sense is no longer at war with soul; the beast is victorious.

The main purport of the Idylls is to show forth the kingship of the soul, and how only through that kingship the beast in man is subdued. Their message is a rebuke to the pride of the flesh, the crime of sense become the crime of malice, the ancient rebellion against the spiritual and God.

THE COMING OF ARTHUR

GUINEVERE, the daughter of King Leodogran, is " the fairest of all flesh on earth." The land of Leodogran is wasted by war from within and from without. Nor law nor peace is there. Internal strife has snapped asunder the bond of rule, and the heathen from without have poured down upon a helpless people.

> For many a petty king ere Arthur came
> Ruled in this isle, and ever waging war
> Each upon other, wasted all the land;
> And still from time to time the heathen host
> Swarmed over seas, and harried what was left.

And so there grew great tracts of wilderness,
Wherein the beast was ever more and more,
And man was less and less, till Arthur came.

Prior to the coming of the spiritual man, war
raged amongst the human passions. Man became
their prey; the passions dominated, and as the
beast in man grew stronger, the man waned less
and less. The victim of his own brutal passions,
he became the easy prey of the heathen from
without. There was no principle of rule, as there
was no principle of unity. The lower nature, having nothing in itself to establish order amongst
its own conflicting elements, dominated not in harmony but in discord. Human society was a waste
and a desolation, where the beast ranged at will.
Here was need of one stronger than the beast.
The spiritual in man must assert its kingship, sub-
jugate the beast, bridle the passions, bring order
out of confusion, and make a realm and reign.

Leodogran, King of Cameliard, knows not
whither to turn for aid, but hearing of Arthur,
newly crowned, sends for him, saying:

. . . . "Arise, and help us, thou
For here between the man and beast we die."

Arthur responds to the appeal, and, coming to the land of Leodogran, there beholds Guinevere, and

> Felt the light of her eyes into his life
> Smite on the sudden, ...
> And passing thence to battle felt
> Travail, and throes and agonies of life,
> Desiring to be joined with Guinevere.

Guinevere is the fairest of all flesh. She, the feminine and receptive element, is symbol of the nobility and beauty of the human body as the destined habitation of the soul. Beautiful should be the tabernacle of the spiritual, a dwelling place in all order and fairness. The soul, the spiritual element, which Arthur typifies, manifests its natural disposition to be united with the body in the human order, for the soul has been made for union with the body.[2] It is a spiritual entity made not to dwell apart, like angelic substance, but with and in the body, the principle of its life and its activities. As Arthur goes to battle he ponders with himself:

> . . . . Her father said
> That here between the man and beast they die.
> Shall I not lift her from this land of beasts
> Up to my throne, and side by side with me?

The human body is not to be left a prey to the
beast; it must be rescued from the despotism of
the brutal passions.   It must be lifted up from
the land of beasts to the very throne of the spiritual.   Here is its proper place, where, by virtue
of its union with the soul, it reigns in comeliness
and power over the world.   On the other hand, how
may the soul fulfill its destined mission without
this intimate union with the body?   What is the
world to it without the body?

> What happiness to reign a lonely king,
> Vext—O ye stars that shudder over me,
> O earth that soundest hollow under me—
> Vext with waste dreams!   For, saving I be joined
> To her that is the fairest under heaven,
> I seem as nothing in the mighty world,
> And cannot will my will, nor work my work
> Wholly, nor make myself in mine own realm
> Victor and lord.   But were I joined with her,
> Then might we live together as one life,
> And, reigning with one will in everything,
> Have power on this dark land to lighten it,
> And power on this dead world to make it live.

Without the body, earth and the things of the
earth are as nothing to the human soul—empty
shadows, waste dreams in the regions of death.

The spiritual principle, the principle of order and rule, is impotent to will its will, to work its work, in a world of matter without that body, which, when one with it, gives it the means of power over earth and the things of earth. To effect the purpose of the soul, that union must be so intimate that the two become really one, that they may reign with one will in everything. This can only be accomplished by lifting the lower nature up to the higher, the spiritual uniting itself with the sensual, infusing its own spiritual fire, its own noble life, into it, and so make the dead world live. Arthur must lift Guinevere up to his throne side by side with him.

In this episode of Arthur coming to the land of Leodogran and there meeting Guinevere in that land of beasts, where he conceives his purpose of taking her to wife, is the ground of the action of the Idylls. In the land of beasts we find sense at war with soul, and sense victorious: the beast in man dominant, the soul in man overcome: discord, confusion, war, chaos, and anarchy supreme. To bring back peace, law, and order, the soul, in union with the body as its vital and controlling element, must subdue the passions and organize human society on a spiritual basis. The accomplishment

of this work is Arthur's mission. The first step
is union with Guinevere.

After Arthur has cleared Leodogran's realm for
him, he sends to the King three chosen knights to
ask for Guinevere's hand:

> Saying, " If I in aught have served thee well,
> Give me thy daughter, Guinevere, to wife."

But Leodogran, after the manner of the flesh,
ever prone to call in question the soul's supremacy,
doubts the kingship of Arthur, and requires con-
firmation of his title. In the pride of the flesh
he will not give his daughter saving to a king who is
also a king's son. In the eyes of the world the legitimacy of Arthur's title was dubious. His own barons had risen against him, disclaiming him as king
of theirs. However much Arthur has helped him
in his need, Leodogran fails to discern the kingly
character of the deed; but measuring the worth of
the savior of his realm by the pride of human birth,
summons his chamberlain, and asks him if he
knows aught of Arthur's origin. The chamberlain refers the King to Bleys and Merlin, two sages,
with whom rests the secret. Bleys was Merlin's
master, but the latter, says Leodogran's chamberlain, so far outstripped his master, that the master

in his turn became the scholar. In Bleys we have
Knowledge typified, in Merlin, Wisdom; for Wisdom, so we read in *In Memoriam*, excels Knowledge:

> . . . Let her know her place:
> She is the second, not the first.
>
> .   .   .   .   .   .
>
> For she is earthly of the mind,
> But wisdom heavenly of the soul.

Merlin is Arthur's great counsellor, building
him his cities and guiding him in the ruling of
his realm. Wisdom is the supreme director of the
soul, and Wisdom alone possesses the secret of its
birth. Knowledge cannot penetrate to the final
causes of things; that is reserved to Wisdom.

It is Merlin who presents Arthur to the quarrel-
ing barons as their king. But they cry out:

> . . . Away with him!
> No king of ours.

The warring passions refuse to submit to the
sovereignty of the soul. The sensual man would
rule according to the flesh in discord and lawlessness. He would rather suffer the strife engendered
by license than submit to the happy bonds by

which spiritual liberty is secured. None knows of
Arthur's birth; nearly all doubt. Some few, as
Bedivere, Ulfius, Brastias and Bellicent, believe in
him as true king, but their acceptance is on faith.
Bedivere's answer to the King's inquiries gives the
latter no assurance. His answer is by faith, not by
knowledge. Whilst Leodogran debates with himself the question of Arthur's legitimacy, his mind
divided in doubt, Queen Bellicent, Lot's wife and
Arthur's reputed sister, comes to his court.
By way of leading up to the main object of his
inquiry, Leodogran asks her if she thinks the
kingdom founded by Arthur possesses stability
and power enough to perpetuate itself. Bellicent
then narrates, as an eye-witness, the scene of the
founding of the Round Table:

. . . Then the King, in low, deep tones,
And simple words of great authority,
Bound them by so strait vows to his own self,
That when they rose knighted from kneeling, some
Were pale as at the passing of a ghost,
Some flushed and others dazed, as one who wakes,
Half-blinded at the coming of a light.

The Round Table is the spiritual organization
of man. A new spirit is breathed into the sensual

man. The new man awakens to a higher life. He
is sworn to a new order of things. He has vowed
himself to the spiritual head and model; and those
whom Arthur, the spiritual man, has bound so
straightly to himself, grow pale when the splendor
and awe of that spiritual world first open to their
vision; some are flushed and others dazed, half-
blinded by the effulgence of light that has burst
upon them. They tremble with apprehension.

> But when he spake and cheered his Table Round
> With large, divine, and comfortable words
> Beyond my tongue to tell thee—I beheld
> From eye to eye thro' all their order flash
> A momentary likeness of the King:
> And ere it left their faces, thro' the cross
> And those around it and the Crucified,
> Down from the casement over Arthur, smote
> Flame color, vert and azure, in three rays,
> And falling upon each of three fair queens,
> Who stood in silence near his throne, the friends
> Of Arthur, gazing on him, tall, with bright
> Sweet faces, who will help him at his need.

Merlin is also described as present:

> And near him stood the Lady of the Lake—
> Who knows a subtler magic than his own—
> Clothed in white samite, mystic, wonderful;

She gave the King his huge cross-hilted sword
Wherewith to drive the heathen out: a mist
Of incense curled about her, and her face
Wellnigh was hidden in the minster gloom;
But there was heard among the holy hymns
A voice as of the waters, for she dwells
Down in a deep calm, whatsoever storms
May shake the world, and when the surface rolls,
Hath power to walk the waters like our Lord.

The meaning of this passage is not hard to discover. It is a picture of the spiritual organization effected by the infusion of Arthur's own spirit
into his knighthood. They become like unto the
King, because they are lifted up by their vows to
his great purpose. As their vows still tremble on
their lips, the three theological virtues, Charity,
Hope, and Faith, appear in the persons of " three
fair queens " amongst them, illumined by three
rays of varied light from above, each in her own
respective symbolical color, red, green, and blue.
This mystic illumination strikes down upon them
from the casement above through the cross and
Him on it, the Crucified, with those around Him,
the pictured scene on the stained-glass window
above Arthur's throne, to signify that it is through
the atonement of Jesus Christ that these three

heavenly virtues, the friends of the soul to help it at its need, come to the aid of the spiritualized man. Merlin, or Wisdom, is also present at the installation of the Round Table, now the type of the spiritualized body, politic and social. But more especially to be noted is the mystic Lady of the Lake, who possesses even a subtler magic than Merlin's. In her Religion is symbolized. She dwells in a deep calm at the bases of the hills, beneath the stormy waters of the world, in her eternal repose, and has power, like her Lord and Founder, to walk the troubled surface of the sea. It is she who gives to Arthur the brand Excalibur wherewith to drive the heathen out; for it is Religion that gives to the soul the spiritual weapons wherewith to war against the passions and hell typified by the heathen. Excalibur is to be used and then returned, but not until the soul quits its earthly tenement; then the soul will have no further need of a weapon, for that moment it passes from the state militant to the state triumphant.

Leodogran is pleased to learn of the great promise of Arthur's kingdom. But Bellicent's account of the Round Table does not solve his doubt of Arthur's legitimacy. When he asks her what she knows of his birth, Bellicent narrates to him the

story of Arthur's coming, which the dying Bleys
had confided to her keeping; how he and Merlin
on the night of Uther's death,

.   .   .   From the castle gateway by the chasm
Descending through the dismal night—a night
In which the bounds of heaven and earth were **lost—**
Beheld, so high upon the dreary deeps
It seemed in heaven, a ship, the shape thereof
A dragon wing'd, and all from stem to stern
Bright with a shining people on the decks,
And gone as soon as seen.   And then the two
Dropt to the cove, and watched the great sea **fall,**
Wave after wave, each mightier than the last,
Till last, a ninth one, gathering half the deep
And full of voices, slowly rose and plunged
Roaring, and all the wave was in a flame;
And down the wave and in the flame was **borne**
A naked babe, and rode to Merlin's feet,
Who stoopt and caught the babe, and cried, " The King!
Here is an heir for Uther!"   And the fringe
Of that great breaker, sweeping up the strand,
Lashed at the wizard as he spoke the word,
And all at once all round him rose in fire,
So that the child and he were clothed in fire.
And presently thereafter followed calm,
Free sky and stars: "And this same child," he **said,**
" **Is he who reigns.**"

Who, then, is Arthur? Surely the babe myste-
riously washed up from the deep is not Uther's
heir? The night of his coming, says Bleys, is one
when the bounds of heaven and earth seem to meet.
His coming is attended by the apparition of a
shining ship, so high upon the deeps that it
seemed in heaven, and whose decks are bright with
a celestial people. Nine great waves, each mightier
than the last, come roaring inward to the shore,
and the ninth sweeps flaming up the strand, bearing a naked babe to Merlin's feet.

This is the advent of the human soul from that
eternity whence it comes to human birth—to the
shores of time. So does the poet sing elsewhere,

> And breaking let the splendor fall
> To spangle all the happy shores,
> By which they rest, and ocean sounds,
> And, star and system rolling past,
> A soul shall draw from out the vast
> And strike his being into bounds.*

It is out of eternity, from amongst the celestial
people on the shining ship, the shape thereof a
dragon winged, the ancient British symbol of sovereignty, that the soul comes into the bounds of

* In Memoriam. cxxxi.

human existence. It comes inswathed in fire, the
symbol of life. Merlin proclaims this babe from
out the deep " The King! " He is King not because he is the heir of Uther's body, but by virtue
of the spiritual supremacy of the soul. It is the
kingship of the higher over the lower nature. And
this is the King, says the dying Bleys, who now
reigns.

When Bellicent questions Merlin as to the truth
of Bleys' story, he answers her in what she terms
" riddling triplets of old times: "

> Rain, rain and sun! a rainbow in the sky!
> A young man will be wiser by and by;
> An old man's wits may wander ere he die.
>
> Rain, rain and sun! a rainbow on the lea!
> And truth is this to me and that to thee;
> And truth or clothed or naked let it be.
>
> Rain, sun and rain! and the free blossom blows!
> Sun, rain and sun! and where is he who knows?
> From the great deep to the great deep he goes.

Bellicent's human curiosity would pierce the
mystery of the soul's origin, and Merlin answers
her in what she calls riddles, because their meaning
is beyond her limited comprehension. Merlin's

triplets cloak a great truth not seen by Bellicent.
Life has its many vicissitudes, its rain and its sun-
shine, storm and calm, hopes and fears, joys and
sorrows, but truth abides unchanging, whether it
be clothed or naked to human eyes. The soul,
which is the house of truth, passes through all
changes of time, all vicissitudes of space, from
eternity to eternity:

From the great deep to the great deep he goes.

Though Merlin's riddling answer angers Bellicent, Wisdom will not unveil an unbearable light to
the weakness of human eyes. For Bellicent, who
stands for the type of those to whom Wisdom knows
better than disclose her profound secrets, faith is
sufficient. She is such an one as may not see the
Holy Grail unveiled. Yet she accepts Arthur on
faith, believing in his kingship, for Merlin, whom
she knows to be Wisdom, has sworn,

Though men may wound him, that he will not die.

So Wisdom pledges itself for the immortality of
the soul, which passes but cannot die.

Leodogran rejoices at Bellicent's account of
Arthur's coming, but is not convinced, and still

weighs the " yea " or " nay" to Arthur's suit,
and, growing drowsy with the perplexity of his
doubt, nods and sleeps, and sees,

> Dreaming, a slope of land that ever grew,
> Field after field, up to a height, the peak
> Haze-hidden, and thereon a phantom king,
> Now looming, and now lost; and on the slope
> The sword rose, the hind fell, the herd was driven.
> Fire glimpsed; and all the land from roof and rick,
> In drifts of smoke before a rolling wind,
> Streamed to the peak, and mingled with the haze
> And made it thicker, while the phantom king
> Sent out at times a voice; and here or there
> Stood one who pointed toward the voice, the rest
> Slew on and burnt, crying, "No king of ours,
> No son of Uther, and no king of ours;"
> Till with a wink his dream was changed, the haze
> Descended and the solid earth became
> As nothing, but the King stood out in heaven,
> Crowned.

Leodogran's dream is a vision of the turmoil
and strife of human life, the fierce war of the
passions clouding the moral atmosphere and bind-
ing men, who in the heat and rage of contest cry
out against their better nature, swearing that the
spiritual man is not to be obeyed. They burn,

destroy, slay, heedless of aught save their own furious purpose. Each would be sovereign, recognizing no law, obeying no ruler. In their disorder they perish. When the battle is over and the dust of contest laid, the smoke and flame of passion passed, the spiritual man stands out in his glory a crowned king, the only abiding presence where all else has vanished.

All Leodogran's doubts are dispelled by his vision. He now recognizes the kingship of the spiritual man. It is no longer a question whether Arthur be Uther's son or not. He has a higher claim to sovereignty than the accident of royal progenitors. He is king by a diviner right than heredity. Sending for Arthur's ambassadors, Leodogran answers " yes " to the King's suit; and so Guinevere is given to Arthur to wife, which twain Dubric, the high saint, weds and blesses, saying:

> Reign ye and love, and make the world
> Other; and may thy Queen be one with thee,
> And all this Order of thy Table Round
> Fulfill the boundless purpose of the King!

Through the union of the flesh with the spirit the world is to become other, men lifted up above the brutish sense, and the spiritual order estab-

lished in the Round Table to work out the boundless purpose of the King.   At the marriage feast
the lords of Rome, the symbol of paganism, the
slowly fading mistress of the world, stand at the
portal of the church gazing in scorn at the scene,
while Arthur's knights proclaim the new order,
singing:

> Blow trumpet, for the world is white with May;
> Blow trumpet, the long night hath rolled away!
> Blow through the living world—Let the King reign!
> .   .   .   .
> The King will follow Christ, and we the King,
> In whom high God had breathed a secret thing.
> Fall battle ax and flash brand!   Let the King reign!

It is the springtime of the new order.[3]   It is
the Easter season, the time of the great resurrec-
tion.   The night has rolled away, and the spiritual
sun has risen in his glory on a world white with
purity and the promise of the flower to come.
Let the spiritual man reign in Christ.   He is our
true king.   Nor Rome nor heathen shall rule where
Arthur reigns, the spiritual man made king in
Christ.

When the great lords of Rome demand tribute,
Arthur answers them, saying:

The old order changeth, yielding place to new;
And we that fight for our fair father Christ,
Seeing that ye be grown too weak and old
To drive the heathen from your Roman wall,
No tribute will we pay.

The reign of pagan Rome is over; a new era
has come in, a new law is established. Hence-
forth men are to be ruled by a spiritual king; the
old allegiance to the world has been severed, and
a new kingdom set up in its place. So Arthur
and his knights strive with Rome, and, through
being one in will,

  . . . In twelve great battles overcame
The heathen hordes and made a realm and reigned.

The spiritual order is now confirmed and Arthur's knights wedded by their vows to the purpose of their King:

To reverence the King as if he were
Their conscience, and their conscience as their King;
To break the heathen and uphold the Christ;
To ride abroad redressing human wrongs;
To speak no slander, no, nor listen to it;
To lead sweet lives in purest chastity;
To love one maiden only, cleave to her,
And worship her by years of noble deeds,
Until they won her.

In this way is to be brought about the cleansing of the realm, the purification of the heart and the strengthening of the will, by restraining and directing the desires to a pure object, and by disciplining them through repeated efforts to the attainment of its ideal. In this way are the passions to be subjected to right reason, not stamped out, but guided to their true and proper object. So man is to attain the perfect harmony of living, the affections and the will tending in unison to the goal of perfection; law, order, and justice reigning in the world through the spiritual man, true king and true lord.

GARETH AND LYNETTE

In *Gareth and Lynette*, the second Idyll, we are shown the development of the individual under the directive influence of the spiritual organization. The story of Gareth may be regarded as an epitome of the theme of the Idylls. It is the history of the human soul in mortal combat with the powers of sense. Gareth is the type of the spiritualized man victorious over time and death.

Gareth is " the last tall son of Lot and Bellicent," the best beloved of his mother, who cherishes
him in fond solicitude apart from the busy ways
of men.   This idle and unprofitable life grows irk-
some to the budding manhood of the restive youth,
in whose bosom flames that unquenchable aspiration of the noble soul to the fame of great deeds
done for the King's sake.   He urges his suit with
more than the keen impetuosity of youth.   The
ardor of his aspiration burns away the natural
bonds of affection; but he yields obedience and
seeks his mother's consent.   She, in her doting love,
would hold him back.   She pictures a life of ease
and safety to him on his ancestral domains " with
some comfortable bride and fair " and amid the
pleasures of the chase.   But this were a life of sloth
and shame to a soul that sees, and will be content
only with the highest:

. . . . Shame!
Man am I grown, a man's work must I do.
Follow the deer?   Follow the Christ, the King,
Live pure, speak true, right wrong, follow the King—
Else, wherefore born?

Seeing that the comforts and allurements of the
senses cannot shake Gareth from his high purpose,

the mother, in the folly of her love, would cast
doubts on Arthur's kingship:

> . . . . . . Wilt thou leave
> Thine easeful biding here, and risk thine all,
> Life, limbs, for one that is not proven King?

But to Gareth, the man of spiritual aspiration,
there is but one test of kingship—the kingly deed:

> Not proven, who swept the dust of ruined Rome
> From off the threshold of the realm, and crushed
> The Idolaters, and made the people free?
> Who should be King save him who makes us free?

So ever runs the answer of the spiritual man;
kingly is as kingly does. Who succors us from
the thraldom of the senses proves his right to reign.
Such is Gareth's indomitable purpose. And his
mother, seeing " her son's will unwaveringly one,"
yields to his importunity on one condition: that
he walk through fire and smoke to the attainment
of his object—he must serve a twelvemonth and a
day as a scullion in Arthur's kitchen. She thinks
the shame of such service will prove too great a
test to her son's pride. But to the spiritual man
the lowlier the service the higher the virtue. Base-
ness is not in the deed, but in the doer. Pride has

no part in him. Humility is the root of his greatness. Gareth, a king's son, is not princely proud, and sooty kitchen vassalage cannot demean him or sully his noble nature. He will serve with scullions and kitchen slaves for the King's sake in all nobleness, for, as he says:

The thrall in person may be free in soul.

With his mother's consent,—he will not go without that consent, for obedience, like humility, is a prime virtue of the spiritual man,—Gareth, with two followers, takes his departure for Camelot, the city where Arthur holds his court. Like the henchmen with him, he is clad as a tiller of the soil; he, a prince royal, in outer semblance as lowly as the lowliest, to teach the high lesson that it is not the outward show that indicates the true man.

. . . When their feet were planted on the plain,
That broadened toward the base of Camelot,
Far off they saw the silver-misty morn
Rolling her smoke about the royal mount
That rose between the forest and the field.
At times the summit of the high city flashed;
At times the spires and turrets half-way down
Pricked thro' the mist; at times the great gate shone
Only, that opened on the field below:
Anon, the whole fair city had disappeared.

Gareth's henchmen grow fearful at the weird appearance of the mystic city, anon flashing through and then vanishing in the shifting mists of morning. They become reluctant to go further, and importune Gareth to turn back home and desert an enterprise where magic seems to play the chief part. But Gareth, laughing at their churlish fears,

> . . . pushed them all unwilling toward the gate,
> And there was no gate like it under heaven;
> For barefoot on the keystone, which was lined
> And rippled like an ever fleeting wave,
> The Lady of the Lake stood; all her dress
> Wept from her sides as water flowing away;
> But, like the cross, her great and goodly arms
> Stretched under all the cornice and upheld;
> And drops of water fell from either hand;
> And down from one a sword was hung, from one
> A censer, either worn with wind and storm;
> And o'er her breast floated the Sacred Fish;
> And in the space to left of her, and right,
> Were Arthur's wars in weird devices done,
> New things and old co-twisted, as if time
> Were nothing, so inveterately, that men
> Were giddy gazing there: and over all
> High on the top were those three queens, the friends
> Of Arthur, who should help him at his need.

The titanic image carved above the gates of the mystic city is Religion, the Lady of the Lake. Through religion do we enter the spiritual city of Camelot. Religion is the gateway to Arthur's court, the house of the soul. The upholding arms of the Lady of the Lake stretched like the cross, the sign of spiritual redemption, signifies the sustaining power of religion in the social and moral order; "stretched under all the cornice and upheld"; the water flowing from her hands signifies baptism and absolution, regeneration and pardon; the suspended sword, the spiritual weapons of the soul; the censer, prayer and sacrifice; the sacred fish, the 'Ιχθύς, the ancient symbol of Christ, formed from the initial letters of the Greek sentence, Jesus Christ, Son of God, Saviour.[4] Arthur's wars, in the spaces to the right and left of her, symbolize the soul's battles with sense and time; the three queens above, Faith, Hope, and Charity, the three theological virtues, crowning all.

As Gareth and his dazed followers stand staring at the great gate, a blast of music sounds, and a gray-bearded sage, type of wisdom, comes out from the city, and inquires who they are. Gareth replies that they are tillers of the soil come to see the glory of Arthur's city, and at the same time begs

the graybeard to convince his skeptical followers
of the city's reality:

> .　.　.　.　.　.　.　These, my men
> (Your city moved so weirdly in the mist),
> Doubt if the King be King at all, or come
> From Fairyland; and whether this be built
> By magic, and by fairy kings and queens;
> Or whether there be any city at all,
> Or all a vision: and this music now
> Hath scared them both; but tell thou these the truth.

Camelot is the spiritual city, *Civitas Dei*, which
the tillers of the earth, cattle of the field, as the old
seer calls them, averred was no real city, but only a
vision. To the sensual man there is but one reality,
and that is matter. What is not visible to the eye,
palpable to the senses, he will not recognize as real.

> Then that old seer made answer, playing on him,
> And saying: "Son, I have seen the good ship sail
> Keel upward and mast downward in the heavens,
> And solid turrets topsy-turvy in air;
> And here is truth."

To those who are sunk in the grossness of their
lower nature, who make their senses the sole cri-
terion of the real and the true, the wonders of the
mirage narrated by the seer are absurd. More won-

derful than these, the higher truth; but how may
they know it who make the brute sense the measure
of all knowledge? Even in these physical phenomena is truth which they cannot perceive.

 . . . . . But an it please thee not,
Take thou the truth as thou hast told it me.
For truly, as thou sayst, a fairy king
And fairy queens have built the city, son;
They came from out a sacred mountain-cleft
Toward the sunrise, each with harp in hand,
And built it to the music of their harps.
And, as thou sayst, it is enchanted, son,
For there is nothing in it as it seems,
Saving the King; tho' some there be that hold
The King a shadow and the city real:
Yet take thou heed of him, for, so thou pass
Beneath this archway, then wilt thou become
A thrall to his enchantments, for the King
Will bind thee by such vows as is a shame
A man should not be bound by, yet the which
No man can keep; but, so thou dread to swear,
Pass not beneath this gateway, but abide
Without, among the cattle of the field.
For an ye heard a music, like enow
They are building still, seeing the city is built
To music, therefore never built at all,
And therefore built forever.

To the sensual man all shadow and magic is this city of the King, the abode of the soul. To him the fleeting phenomena of sense are the only realities, and Ixion-like he embraces the image, not the substance, of truth. Not of brick and mortar is builded this city of God, but of the invisible virtues of the soul, and it is built to music, to that divine harmony of order which keeps the perfect concord of truth and beauty and love in the spiritual kingdom; and it is ever building, and therefore built forever, for this kingdom of the soul is an institution wherein souls are ever being edified unto perfection. In this city is nothing real saving the soul, all else being but type and shadow. Who enters this city must swear the King's vows, uttermost obedience to the King, and to lead sweet lives of purest chastity, vows which it is a shame for a man not to swear, but vows which no man, simply as man, can keep; for he can fulfill them only by becoming spiritualized. Let him who dreads to swear, pass not beneath the mystic archway which gives entrance to the spiritual city, but abide without amongst the cattle of the field, who know only the things of sense. The spiritual kingdom is entered only through Religion. Who refuses to enter therein dwells amongst the brutes, never knowing truth. Gareth, not

comprehending the veiled truth which the old seer
utters, and thinking that he is being mocked,
flashes into anger and retorts indignantly, upbraiding the sage for mocking one who had spoken
him fair. The old man replies:

> Know ye not, then, the riddling of the bards?
> " Confusion, and illusion, and relation,
> Elusion, and occasion, and evasion?"
> I mock thee not but as thou mockest me.
>
> .   .   .   .   .   .
>
> And now thou goest up to mock the King,
> Who cannot brook the shadow of any lie.

You, dwellers with the cattle in the fields, who are
blinded to the spiritual nature of things, do but take
the words of truth after the manner of your own
affliction, blindly. The truth seems confusion and
illusion to you, who regard it as a lie. It is not I
who mock you, but yourselves mocking the truth are
the victims of your own mockery. That clear and
limpid surface returns your own distorted image
faithfully to you, but because it reflects your own
dreadful features so accurately, you are loath to believe that there is truth in it. To admit that truth
is to confess your own deformity. But he who

would enter into the spiritual city must first see himself as he really is, and so learn to cleanse himself from all taint of untruth. Unless he be so purified, the spiritual city will be but an illusion and a mockery to him.

After Gareth has served a term in sooty kitchen vassalage as a scullion at the King's court, that is, after he has been profoundly exercised in the virtues of humility and obedience, the true cornerstones of the spiritual life, he is at last knighted and given a quest by the King, much to the disgust of Kay the Seneschal, who saw not the noble soul under the disguise of the kitchen knave. At this time the damsel Lynette comes to Arthur's court to persuade Sir Lancelot to undertake a quest against four redoubtable knights who hold her sister, Lyonors, a prisoner in the Castle Perilous, around which, in three loops, runs a rapid river. At each of the passes of this three-looped stream abides one of the four knights to guard the ford against all comers; the fourth dwells unseen under the castle walls in the horror of a mysterious silence. Gareth is granted the quest, to the confusion and indignation of the petulant Lynette, who had asked for Arthur's greatest and most renowned knight, Lancelot. Lynette, type of the vanity of the world, can see no virtue in lowliness, and estimates human worth by human appearances.

> . . . And lightly was her slender nose
> Tip-tilted like the petal of a flower.

When Arthur grants the quest to Gareth, his scullion, she rides away in anger, rankling under the affront she deems the King has put on her. Gareth follows, ever answering her scorn and reviling with courtesy and patience, too noble in soul to heed the petulant bickering of worldly vanity or the flouting of injured pride.

After an adventure with bandits, in which Gareth shows his prowess, which but piques Lynette to keener railing, accounting his success mere mishap and mischance, for the world is loath to acknowledge virtue where it has seen only lowliness, they approach the first pass, guarded by the first knight of the mysterious brotherhood. The banks of the stream are rough, thicketed and steep, the stream itself full and narrow:

> . . . . And on the further side
> Arose a silk pavilion, gay with gold
> In streaks and rays, and all Lent-lily in hue,
> Save that the dome was purple, and above
> Crimson, a slender banneret fluttering.

The guardian of this pass calls himself the
Morning Star. At his command three maidens
"in gilt and rosy raiment," whom he terms
Daughters of the Dawn, approach and arm him.

These arm'd him in blue arms, and gave a shield
Blue also, and thereon the Morning Star.
And Gareth silent gazed upon the knight,
Who stood a moment, ere his horse was brought,
Glorying; and in the stream beneath him, shone,
Immingled with Heaven's azure waveringly,
The gay pavilion and the naked feet,
His arms, the rosy raiment, and the star.

   .   .   .   .   .

. . . And all at fiery speed the two
Shock'd on the central bridge, and either spear
Bent, but not brake, and either knight at once,
Hurl'd as a stone from out a catapult
Beyond his horse's crupper and the bridge,
Fell, as if dead, but quickly rose and drew;
And Gareth lash'd so fiercely with his brand,
He drove his enemy backward down the bridge,
The damsel crying, "Well-stricken, kitchen knave!"
Till Gareth's shield was cloven; but one stroke
Laid him that clove it groveling on the ground.

The Knight of the Morning Star symbolizes
Youth, and the gay pavilion, in which he dwells with

his maidens in rosy raiment, is the abode of pleasure.
Youth, the season of pleasure, with its temptations, guards the first pass of the river of life, here
swift and narrow, which the spiritual man in his
mortal journey must cross. Barring his way is the
Knight of the Morning Star. Him must the spiritual man vanquish. Nor is this accomplished at
the first onset, nor without fierce struggle. Not
until the Knight of the Morning Star, who is
strong with the wine of pleasure, is brought groveling to the ground is victory assured. Then is he
at the mercy of the spiritual man, who sends him to
Arthur's court, there to serve, not in wantonness
and lawlessness, but in virtue and subjection to the
King.

Upon Gareth's victory, Lynette, though still reviling the victor, sings:

> O morning star (not that tall felon there
> Whom thou, by sorcery or unhappiness
> Or some device, hast foully overthrown),
> O morning star that smilest in the blue,
> O star, my morning dream hath proven true;
> Smile sweetly, thou! my love hath smiled on me.

It is as the messenger of the imprisoned Lady
Lyonors that Lynette sings the first victory of the

soul over sense. It is not the morning star of
pleasure, not the conquered felon overthrown by
Gareth, whom she salutes, but the morning star of
the spiritual world, now risen resplendent in the
dawn, and presaging the final victory to come.

At the second loop the Noonday Sun stands
guard against their passage:

Huge, on a huge red horse, and all in mail
Burnished to blinding, shone the Noonday Sun
Beyond a raging shallow.   As if the flower,
That blows a globe of after arrowlets,
Ten thousand-fold had grown, flashed the fierce shield,
All sun; and Gareth's eyes had flying blots
Before them when he turned from watching him.
.   .   .   .

"Ugh!" cried the Sun, and vizoring up a red
And cipher face of rounded foolishness,
Push'd horse across the foamings of the ford,
Whom Gareth met midstream: no room was there
For lance or tourney skill: four strokes they struck
With sword, and these were mighty; the new knight
Had fear he might be shamed; but as the Sun
Heaved up a ponderous arm to strike the fifth,
The hoof of his horse slipt in the stream, the stream
Descended, and the Sun was washed away.

The Noonday Sun, ablaze with a blinding light,
is the season of middle age, glowing fierce with the

ambitions of the world. He guards the second loop
of the river of life, barring its ford, a raging shallow, against the passage of the spiritual man. His
" cipher face of rounded foolishness " is emblematic
of the folly of ambition, the " vanity of vanities,
and all is vanity," of the wise King of Holy Writ.
Sharp and rough the battle with him, blow for blow,
buffet for buffet, until he goes under, by the over-
balance of his own huge strength, in the slippery
shallows of the stream he would hold against the
spiritual man.

Again Lynette sings:

O Sun (not this strong fool whom thou, Sir Knave,
Hast overthrown thro' mere unhappiness),
O Sun, that wakenest all to bliss or pain,
O Moon, that layest all to sleep again,
Shine sweetly; twice my love hath smiled on me.

The glory of the spiritual man's victory of the
morn has now risen to mid-day splendor. He who
has conquered the passions of youth is victorious
over the harsher temptations of middle age. The
sun of his victory shines resplendent in the mid-
heavens. Twice has he conquered, and the promise
of final victory grows in brightness.

At the third loop the Knight of the Evening
Star stands guard. He is clothed in hardened
skins, that fit him like his own. These, says Lynette, will turn the sword even if his armor be cleaved
from him. Gareth declares that the same strength
which threw the Morning Star can throw the Evening Star.

Then that other blew

A hard and deadly note upon the horn.
"Approach and arm me!" With slow steps from out
An old storm-beaten, russet, many-stained
Pavilion, forth a grizzled damsel came,
And arm'd him in old arms, and brought a helm
With but a drying evergreen for crest,
And gave a shield whereon the Star of Even,
Half tarnished and half bright, his emblem, shone.
But when it glittered o'er the saddle bow,
They madly hurled together on the bridge;
And Gareth overthrew him, lighted, drew,
There met him drawn, and overthrew him again,
But up like fire he started; and as oft
As Gareth brought him groveling on his knees,
So many a time he vaulted up again,
Till Gareth panted hard, and his great heart,
Foredooming all his trouble was in vain,
Labored within him, for he seemed as one
That all in later, sadder age, begins
To war against ill uses of a life,

But these from all his life arise, and cry,
" Thou hast made us lords, and canst not put us down."

It is in the figure here that we have the literal
truth. The Knight of the Evening Star is old age,
encased in the toughened habits of a lifetime, fit-
ting like a hardened skin as close as his own. Who
has not overcome the passions of youth, conquered
the ambitions of manhood, will not subdue the
vicious uses of a lifetime that have become a second
nature in old age. He wars against the ill uses of
a life that have become his masters. But, as Gareth
declares, the strength that threw the Morning Star
can throw the Evening Star:

. . . . Till at length Gareth's brand
Clashed his, and brake it utterly to the hilt.
" I have thee now!" but forth that other sprang,
And all unknightlike, writhed his wiry arms
Around him, till he felt, despite his mail,
Strangled, but, straining ev'n his uttermost,
Cast, and so hurl'd him headlong o'er the bridge
Down to the river, sink or swim.

The virtue which overcame the Morning Star has
overthrown the Evening Star. Thrice has victory
shone on the spiritual man. He is conqueror at

the third loop of life's river, where the current
flows broad and deep.   Again Lynette sings:

> O trefoil, sparkling on the rainy plain,
> O rainbow with three colors after rain,
> Shine sweetly: thrice my love hath smiled on me.

Gareth's threefold victory has at last beaten
down Lynette's worldly prejudices.   She confesses
her shame at having reviled him.   She thought the
King had scorned her and hers in sending one so
ignoble on the quest, when she had asked for the
noblest.   Gareth replies simply that she should not
have doubted the King: "You said your say, mine
answer was the deed."   Let the world revile as it
may, the deed is the answer of the spiritual man in
the service of the King.   Lynette now conducts the
thrice victorious Gareth to a cave hard by, provided
by Lady Lyonors with meat and wine for her coming champion:

> Anon they past a narrow comb, wherein
> Were slabs of rock with figures, knights on horse
> Sculptured and deckt in slowly-waning hues.
> "Sir Knight, my knight, a hermit once was here,
> Whose holy hand hath fashioned on the rock
> The war of time against the soul of man.

And yon four fools have sucked their allegory
From these damp walls, and taken but the form.
Know ye not these?" And Gareth lookt and read,

.   .   .   .

" Phosphorus," then " Meridies,"—" Hesperus"—
" Nox "—" Mors," beneath five figures, armed men
Slab after slab, their faces forward all,
And running down the Soul, a Shape that fled
With broken wings, torn raiment and loose hair,
For help and shelter to the hermit's cave.

This passage not only sounds the keynote of the
present Idyll in particular, but gives us the motif
of the entire Round Table series. The Soul in its
journey through Time is assailed by all the powers
of Sense, by the temptations of the flesh in youth,
by the allurements of pride in middle age, and in
old age by the vicious habits engendered by the past
indulgence of both. Pursued by the powers of evil
the Soul flies for help and shelter to the hermit's
cave, where alone she finds succor against her foes.
The truth shines through the allegory. It is in
the spiritual life that the Soul finds consolation and
strength to battle against the powers that would
destroy her. Lynette says that the four knights—
fools, she calls them—against whom Gareth has

undertaken the quest, have sucked their allegory from the sculpture on the walls of the hermit's cave. Lynette, still looking with the eyes of the world, sees only a fool's allegory in the conduct of the four knights who guard the passes of the river and hold the Lady Lyonors prisoner. But it is the figure of the actual warfare which Sense wages against Soul. Just as Lynette fails to recognize the true nobility of Gareth under his humble garb of scullion, and only admits it after the success of his arms forces her to bow to established merit, so now she sees only the exterior fashion of the truth. It is a fool's allegory, after all. The world is blind to the warfare waged by the powers of Sense against the Soul.

There yet remains another knight for Gareth to overthrow before the Lady Lyonors is free; he is the fourth knight of the allegory, sometimes called Nox and sometimes Mors. He is huge of limb and boundless savagery. Lynette says of him:

> God wot, I never looked upon the face,
> Seeing he never rides abroad by day;
> But watched him have I like a phantom pass
> Chilling the night: nor have I heard the voice.
> Always he made his mouthpiece of a page
> Who came and went, and still reported him

As closing in himself the strength of ten,
And when his anger tare him, massacring
Man, woman, lad and girl—yea, the soft babe!

But Gareth is nothing daunted by the terror of
Lynette's description of his antagonist. Lynette
trembles with fear as they approach the walls of
Castle Perilous, and Lancelot, who meantime has
joined them, feels a chill strike through his blood.

And all the three were silent, seeing, pitched
Beside the Castle Perilous on flat field,
A huge pavilion like a mountain peak
Sunder the glooming crimson of the marge,
Black, with black banner, and a long black horn
Beside it hanging, which Sir Gareth grasped,
And so, before the two could hinder him,
Sent all his heart and breath thro' all the horn.
.   .   .   .

.   .   .   .   .   . But when the Prince
Three times had blown, after long hush, at last
The huge pavilion slowly yielded up,
Thro' those black foldings, that which housed therein.
High on a nightblack horse, in nightblack arms,
With white breast-bone, and barren ribs of Death,
And crown'd with fleshless laughter, some ten steps,
In the half light, thro' the dim dawn, advanced
The monster, and then paused and spake no word.

Gareth and Death hurl together:

Then those that did not blink the terror, saw
That Death was cast to ground, and slowly rose.
But with one stroke Sir Gareth split the skull.
Half fell to right and half to left and lay.
Then with a stronger buffet he clove the helm
As throughly as the skull; and out from this
Issued the bright face of a blooming boy
Fresh as a flower new-born, and crying, "Knight,
Slay me not: my three brethren bade me do it,
To make a horror all about the house,
And stay the world from Lady Lyonors.
They never dreamed the passes would be past."

So the spiritual man who has overcome Pleasure, Ambition, and their ill uses, by that same strength overthrows Death. The ghastly imageries of Death do not appall him, for death has fears for him only who has misused life. The powers of Sense had hoped to hold the Soul, whom Lady Lyonors here symbolizes, prisoner against the coming of the spiritual man. They never dreamed the passes would be passed. If the powers of Sense be suffered to usurp all the uses of life the Soul is held in bondage, and Death rides triumphant in all the ghastly imageries of that which Life has done with. It is

the knightly quest of the spiritual man to combat
and overcome these evil powers. Victory over
them makes victory over Death easy. So is Death
stripped of all its terrors, and only dreadful in the
foolish fears of the slaves of Sense:

> Then sprang the happier day from underground;
> And Lady Lyonors and her house, with dance
> And revel and song, made merry over Death,
> As being, after all their foolish fears
> And horrors, only proven a blooming boy.

A happier day and a new life rise for the soul
upon the victory of the spiritual man. Freed from
the despotism of Sense and the terror of Death the
new order is established and the King reigns.

GERAINT AND ENID

IN *Geraint and Enid* we hear the first note of
discord in the city built to music by Arthur. As yet
the trouble is the mere shadow of that sin of sense
which is to undo the great work of the King. It
is a brief cloud blown across an open sky, presaging
the distant storm, and, for the instant, shadowing
the summer glory of the happy fields below and

hushing the song of birds.   Geraint, who had
wedded Enid, daughter of old Earl Yniol, brought
his wife to court, and there rejoiced to see the common love between Enid and the Queen.

> But when a rumor rose about the Queen,
> Touching her guilty love for Lancelot,
> Tho' yet there lived no proof, nor yet was heard
> The world's loud whisper breaking into storm,

not less Geraint believed it; and there fell

> A horror on him, lest his gentle wife,
> Through that great tenderness for Guinevere,
> Had suffered or should suffer any taint
> In nature.

It was Lancelot who had gone to Leodogran's
court to escort Guinevere to King Arthur. Though
the betrothed of the King, her fancy was snared by
" the warmth and color " she found in Arthur's
chief knight. [" That pure severity of perfect
light " in the spiritual man she imagined too high
for her, and so suffered herself to descend to the
lesser man.) It was the rumor of this guilty love
that led Geraint to withdraw from court and take
Enid with him to his own land. There he sinks
into uxorious idleness, forgetful of his promise to

the King to cleanse his marches of bandit earls and
caitiff knights.   Enid reproaches herself as the
cause of her husband's idleness, now become the
common talk of his people.   Waking from sleep one
morning, Geraint overhears her, in the poignancy
of her self-upbraiding, accusing herself:

O me, I fear that I am no true wife!

His fancy, haunted by the rumor of the Queen's
guilt, flashes into unknightly suspicion of his wife's
faithfulness.   Seized by the rough passion of the
moment, he rushes off into the wilderness on a
bootless quest, compelling Enid to accompany him
appareled in her " worst and meanest dress," in
which he had wooed her in the midst of broken for-
tunes.

In this episode of Geraint's jealous madness we
see how the taint of Guinevere's sin brings its bitter-
ness, the first dread fruits of the poison of the flesh
to innocent hearts, and throws its baleful shadow
over the happiness of guiltless souls.) Geraint rides
madly, venting his rough mood upon the meek Enid,
whom he commands to absolute silence, and stub-
bornly refuses, in the sullen wrath of his unjust
suspicion, to ask her aught of explanation of her

reproachful words.   After various encounters with
lawless knights, they happen upon the realm of Earl
Doorm.   Wounded in the combat with the followers of the riotous Limours, Geraint, overcome by the
heat of the noonday sun, suddenly sinks uncon-
scious from his horse on a bank of grass by the road-
side.   Here Earl Doorm finds him with Enid wailing by his side, and orders him to be carried to his
castle hall.   Earl Doorm is the antithesis of King
Arthur, and his riotous following the loathsome
opposite of the Round Table.   His is the household
of the flesh.   It is a scene of lawlessness, riot, and
confusion.

But in the falling afternoon returned
The huge Earl Doorm with plunder to the hall.
His lusty spearmen followed him with noise:
Each hurling down a heap of things that rang
Against the pavement, cast his lance aside,
And doffed his helm; and then there fluttered in
Half-bold, half-frighted, with dilated eyes,
A tribe of women, dress'd in many hues,
And mingled with the spearmen: And Earl Doorm
Struck with a knife's haft hard against the board,
And call'd for flesh and wine to feed his spears;
And men brought in whole hogs and quarter beeves,
And all the hall was dim with steam of flesh:

And none spake word, but all sat down at once,
And ate with tumult in the naked hall,
Feeding like horses when you hear them feed;
Till Enid shrank far back into herself,
To shun the wild ways of the lawless tribe.

Earl Doorm would force Enid to eat and drink,
and offers to make her the mistress of his lawless
household, one with the creatures around his board,
gay with the meretricious splendor of their shame.
Upon Enid's loathing refusal, the ruffian smites
her on the cheek, and at her plaintive cry, Geraint,
having regained consciousness, starts up, and with
one stroke severs Doorm's head from his body.
Amidst the consternation and confusion that follow, Geraint and Enid take to horse and escape,
and meet Arthur on his way to deliver judgment
against the lawless earl.

Geraint's unworthy suspicion of Enid's faith,
his obstinate pride, urging him to a foolish quest,
wherein he brought shame and danger to Enid with
both the lawless Limours and the brutal Doorm,
were evidence of a man not fully spiritualized, of a
knight who had not become complete master of himself. Arthur rebukes him for his headlong quest,
which he had undertaken, not for the King's cause

and the sake of justice, but out of the caprice of his
own narrow and falsely jealous pride. Who con-
quers himself, says the King, is the true Knight of
the Round Table.

> A thousandfold more great and wonderful
> Than if some knight of mine, risking his life,
> My subject with my subjects under him,
> Should make an onslaught single on a realm
> Of robbers, tho' he slew them one by one,
> And were himself nigh wounded to the death.

In Edyrn, Geraint's former rival, whom the latter had overthrown in the height of his pride, we see
one who has by grace and will plucked " the vicious
quitch of blood and custom wholly out of him."
After his overthrow by Geraint, he learns the essential lessons of humility and obedience at Arthur's
court, and becomes one of the noblest, most valorous,
sanest, and most obedient of the King's knights.
In the story of Geraint and Enid we see the be-
ginnings of the tragedy which culminates in the
destruction of the Round Table. As yet the evil
has not taken visible shape; it is still a mere rumor.

> . . . . . Not yet was heard
> The world's loud whisper breaking into storm.

But it is the shadow of sin falling upon blameless souls, the black passion of the flesh gathering the wrath of the storm to come. Its breath has passed over the tranquil surface of pure souls and shatters the calm image of heaven mirrored there. Geraint suffers through the noisome presence of Lancelot's sin. Its dark shadow has driven the sunlight from his soul, and, not being fully spiritualized, the evil seed strikes bitter root in his heart. In the gross household of Earl Doorm we discover a picture of the very antithesis of the Round Table. Here the sensual man has full sway; his unbridled passions are the ruling forces of his soul, and he passes his years in riot and confusion, all law broken to whim and caprice and sin. It is a picture of all that obtains where the spiritual man does not reign.

BALIN AND BALAN

In *Balin and Balan* we are introduced to a still darker phase of the tragedy, which had for the moment so deeply engloomed the lives of Geraint and Enid. It marks the transition of the sin of sense into the sin of malice in the baleful appearance of Vivien upon the scene, tempting and urging

on the distraught Balin to his own destruction.
Sir Balin, whose savage nature is wont to flame into
sudden heats of passion, seeks to overcome the violence of his disposition under the courtly discipline
of Arthur's hall:

> . . . . . .   And all the knights
> Approved him, and the Queen, and all the world
> Made music, and he felt his being move
> In music with his Order and the King.

But chancing one day upon Sir Lancelot and the
Queen he sees the more than courtesy that passes
between them, and is awakened to a suspicion of the
faithlessness of the two noblest and highest in
Arthur's court.

> . . .   And in him gloom on gloom
> Deepened: he sharply caught his lance and shield,
> Nor stayed to crave permission of the King,
> But, mad for strange adventure, dashed away.

After his adventure at King Pellam's court—
wherein we have a picture of the external show of
spirituality without its soul [5]—Balin comes upon
Vivien in the forest. Under the subtle malice of
her words, pouring the poison of calumny into his
already suspicious soul, she rouses him to a blind
fury:

She ceased; his evil spirit upon him leapt;
He ground his teeth together, sprang with a yell,
Tore from the branch, and cast on earth, the shield,
Drove his mailed heel athwart the royal crown,
Stamped all into defacement, hurl'd it from him
Among the forest weeds, and cursed the tale,
The told-of, and the teller.

His brother, Sir Balan, riding in quest of Sir
Garlon, the invisible knight who slew others un-
aware, takes Sir Balin, now without his shield, for
the "Wood Devil" he came to quell. The brothers
rush together in onset and either slays the other,
while Vivien rides mockingly away.[6] The beast
in the man let loose in Sir Balin's breast, awakened
by the apprehension of the faithlessness of Guinevere and Sir Lancelot, throws off all restraint
under the lash of Vivien's words, and blindly hurls
itself and others to destruction.

MERLIN AND VIVIEN [7]

In *Merlin and Vivien,* the subtlest and most
highly wrought of the Idylls, is brought into view
still another element working to the destruction of

the spiritual order. Heretofore we have seen only the sin of sense diffusing its poison through the membership of the Round Table. Envy and treachery, the sin of sense become the sin of malice, now begin their work of undermining the spiritual foundations of Arthur's kingdom. Mark, King of Cornwall, "the scorn of Arthur and his Table," is the type of the crime of malice, as Doorm is the exemplar of the lawless brutal passions. The exalted ideal of purity and justice, the spiritual standard to which Arthur swore his knights with such straight vows, stirred the vilest dregs of Mark's vicious nature to seething hatred. The height to which he could not climb he railed against, the virtue he possessed not he mocked and scoffed at, and doubted all men pure, who knew himself impure:

. . . . . This Arthur pure!
Great Nature, through the flesh herself hath made,
Gives him the lie! There is no being pure,
My cherub. Saith not Holy Writ the same?

The wily Vivien, a creature of his own craft, to whom, as to Mark, virtue was but the mask of vice, a soul fashioned after Mark's own malicious will, a scoffer and a hater of purity, her,—too willing tool

of the Cornish King's malice,—Mark instigates to
go to Arthur's court to spread the contagion of her
vileness.

   . . . Here are snakes within the grass;
And you, methinks, O Vivien, save ye fear
The monkish manhood, and the mask of pure
Worn by this court, can stir them till they sting.

Vivien makes her boast:

   . . . . I bring thee back,
When I have ferreted out their burrowings,
The hearts of all this Order in mine hand—
Ay—so that fate and craft and folly close,
Perchance, one curl of Arthur's golden beard.

So Vivien seeks Arthur's court and there
subtly, cunningly, treacherously spreads her toils
for the Knights of the Round Table, and even seeks
to tempt the blameless King himself.

   . . . Then as Arthur in the highest
Leaven'd the world, so Vivien in the lowest,
Arriving at a time of golden rest,
And sowing one ill hint from ear to ear,
While all the heathen lay at Arthur's feet,
And no quest came, but all was joust and play,
Leaven'd his hall.   They heard and let her be.

Vivien, balked in her malicious design, withdraws from court. But, not to be thwarted, she sets herself with infinite guile to ensnare Merlin:

> And after that she set herself to gain
> Him, the most famous man of all those times.

Merlin is the type of wisdom, the eyes of the soul. He is the argus-eyed sage guarding the treasures of the spiritual kingdom. If Vivien can but put him to sleep under the charm of woven paces and waving hands, then will she have worked her work and gained her end. For, until Merlin be overcome, in vain do the powers of sense or malice assault the spiritual kingdom.

> Then fell on Merlin a great melancholy;
> He walked with dreams and darkness, and he found
> A doom that ever poised itself to fall,
> An ever-moaning battle in the mist,
> World-war of dying flesh against the life,
> Death in all life, and lying in all love,
> The meanest having power upon the highest
> And the high purpose broken by the worm.

Here is wisdom foreseeing the wrath of the time to come, sown by the sins of the present. In the mirror of his prescience, Merlin sees reflected dimly the dreadful image of the monster spawn of the Queen's unfaithfulness, and the presage of his own doom in the gloom of that dreadful shadow.

Vivien follows Merlin in his dark mood to the woods of Broceliande, and there plies the sage with all her wiles to extort from him the secret of the charm of woven paces and waving hands, giving power, to whomsoever uses it, to put him into a deep sleep, wherein he lies as dead to all save the one who exercises the secret charm. In the episode between Merlin and Vivien we see the world-old story of Samson and Delilah, Solomon and the corrupter of his wisdom. Flattering, cajoling, playing upon his pity, praying a compensating word for her injured innocence, sighing over her abused virtue, which she has too confidingly intrusted to him, abandoning herself to his honor, throwing herself on his mercy, petulant, playful, prayerful, tearful, meek, indignant, now all passion and now all ice, now letting her lissome beauty burst glorious in the sunlight of her smile, now making it rainbow through the lucent tears that his harsh upbraiding draws from the fountains of her melted eyes, she at last wrests the fateful secret from him, overtalked and overworn:

> . . . And what should not have been had been,
> For Merlin, overtalked and overworn,
> Had yielded, told her all the charm, and slept.
> Then, in one moment, she put forth the charm
> Of woven paces and of waving hands,
> And in the hollow oak he lay as dead,
> And lost to life and use and name and fame.

The charm of woven paces and waving hands is that sensual draught of forgetfulness which brings Lethe upon the soul that has once relaxed its vigilance over its higher faculties and has become immersed in the things of sense. Merlin has yielded: the wisdom, upon whose vigilance the integrity of the spiritual kingdom depends, has been put to sleep. Vivien, the masked image of Mark's hate, the personification of the crime of sense become the crime of malice, lust become hate, has extinguished the light of wisdom in the soul and sown the death to come. Of herself she says:

> . . . . Born from death was I
> Among the dead and sown upon the wind.

She would drag down to her own vile level the pure and virtuous even as the hags in Doorm's

household would have helped him to **drag** Enid
down:

. . . Whose souls, the old serpent long had drawn
Down as the worm draws in the withered leaf
And makes it earth.

LANCELOT AND ELAINE

Now that the light of wisdom has been extinguished in the soul, the deadly work of corruption
goes on more rapidly.

In the story of Elaine, the darkness that is slowly
drawing near Arthur's court grows deeper as the
Queen's sin spreads its poison amongst the Knights
of the Round Table. Its somber gloom had fallen
athwart the lives of Geraint and Enid to cloud them
but not to blast them. Upon the innocent Elaine
the black thunderbolt fell and killed. She loved
Lancelot, the guilty lover of the guilty Queen, from
whose crime of sense issued the sin of malice, bringing that corruption which is death. Lancelot had
won in tourney eight of the nine diamonds plucked
from the crown of the dead king chanced upon by
Arthur beside the lonely tarn. These the King had
set up as prizes to be jousted for, one every year:

For so, by nine years' proof, we needs must learn
Which is our mightiest, and ourselves shall grow
In use of arms and manhood, till we drive
The heathen, who, some say, shall rule the land
Hereafter, which God hinder.

Did he win the ninth, Lancelot designed to present the Queen with the completed circlet. But the
ninth proves a baleful prize for Arthur's chiefest
knight, for, attending the lists in disguise, that not
the prowess of his name but sheer skill of arms may
win for him, he is gravely wounded. Elaine nurses
him through the long sickness of his wound, and
through her gentle care brings him back to life from
the shadows of death. Her innocence, her beauty,
her purity, and her sweet tenderness half win him
from his guilty passion.

And peradventure had he seen her first
She might have made this and that other world
Another world for the sick man; but now
The shackles of an old love straitened him,
His honor rooted in dishonor stood,
And faith unfaithful made him falsely true.

Lancelot's sin clings to him like some poisonous
vine to the oak, stifling all the sturdy growth of his
manhood and sending its noisome humor into his

blood. He rejects the pure love of Elaine for the
unhallowed passion of Guinevere, and loves not as
the King had ordained his knights should love. So
the Queen's false love undoes the work of the Round
Table, and Arthur's nearest and best prove traitors
to his house.

The death of Elaine and the petulant jealousy of
the Queen drive the sword of remorse deep into
Lancelot's soul. He wrestles with the demon of his
sin, a noble soul fighting a great vice:

> For what am I ?   What profits me my name
> Of greatest knight ?   I fought for it, and have it:
> Pleasure to have it, none; to lose it, pain;
> Now grown a part of me: but what use in it ?
> To make men worse by making my sin known,
> Or sin seem less, the sinner seeming great ?

But Lancelot does not come out victor in the
struggle with himself. Name and fame, trumpeted
in men's mouths, are yet dear to him, and he has not
the spiritual hardihood to pluck the vice out of his
blood that holds him in guilty bondage to the
Queen. Instead of wresting himself with violence
from his passion, he weakly puts his will in the
Queen's keeping. If she will it, then will he
consent to break the bonds that so defame him.

Lancelot is not spiritualized enough to be free. In spite of his great effort to release himself from this degrading dominion of passion, the vacillating effort of a half desire to hold to his sin keeps him an ignoble prisoner to his shame.

So the current of iniquity sweeps onward, broadening as it flows, its bitter source the poisoned fount of the Queen's guilty love. All that fair life, builded up to the music of order and justice into the spiritual city, is seeping into ruins. The canker is eating into the heart of the Round Table. First comes Geraint's foolish trouble, nearly wrecking his own and Enid's happiness. Then out of the dead fruit of Guinevere's unholy passion, like the worm out of corruption, is begot the crime of malice, and Vivien throws the fatal toils of her treachery about the soul, putting wisdom, its sentinel, to sleep forever. Elaine falls a pure victim to its blight. She comes to Camelot in the silence of death, "like a star in blackest night," bearing mute testimony to the death to come that has been sown by that fatal sin of sense.

> So Arthur bade the meek Sir Percivale
> And pure Sir Galahad to uplift the maid,
> And reverently they bore her into hall.
> Then came the fine Gawain and wondered at her

And Lancelot later came and mused at her,
And last the Queen herself and pitied her.

Elaine's pure love, slain by that guilty love of
Lancelot, is the first deadly fruit of Guinevere's
failure to love the highest when she saw it. And
all the court wondered at her, the fine Gawain,
light o' love, and Lancelot, knowing his own sin
to be the cause of this fair lily's blight, and the
Queen, whose jealous passion had raged against
her, whose purity in death shone so fair beside
Guinevere's soiled splendor; but none may touch
her, save the meek Sir Percivale and the pure Sir
Galahad. And her coming was a silent judgment
upon the Queen and Lancelot, the fairness of her
purity a reproach to the blackness of their sin
" like a star in blackest night."

THE HOLY GRAIL

NONE may see the Holy Grail but the utterly
pure. Whomsoever sin has tainted, or the love of
earthly things holds in bondage, to him the Holy
Cup, symbol of spiritual contemplation, will never
be manifest.[9]

Of all Arthur's knights, most of whom rashly

swore the vow of the quest of the Holy Grail, but
one saw fully, and but two caught a fleeting glimpse
of the Sacred Object.   The King upbraids his
knights for their rash presumption in swearing to
undertake a quest beyond their powers.   Such a
quest becomes Sir Galahad, a knight of utter
purity, and Percivale ranging next to him, but it
is not given to everyone to pursue that high vision
till its rapt ecstasy snatch him up to the City of
the Saints.

"What are ye ?   Galahads ?   No, nor Percivales."
    .   .   .   "Nay," said he, "but men
With strength and will to right the wronged, of power
To lay the sudden heads of violence flat,
Knights that in twelve great battles splashed and dyed
The strong White Horse in his own heathen blood—
But one hath seen, and all the blind will see."

In this kingdom of the Soul it is not for all to be
contemplatives, to transcend the active life in vision
of the unveiled truth.   The few alone become so
perfectly spiritualized as to see the truth unveiled.
It is in the active life that most are called to work
out their perfection, and rash and presumptuous is
he who would follow the Holy Grail, deserting the
work at hand when not expressly called to the
higher life.

Sir Galahad, whom "God had made as good as he was beautiful," is the perfectly spiritualized man, who sees the vision, and, rapt in ecstasy, follows it and passes to the higher life. Sir Percivale, who also undertakes the Holy Quest, sees the Holy Grail only after he has been cleansed of the sins that stain his soul. He had not lost himself to find himself as Galahad, and not until he had purged his soul of self and donned the lowly garment of humility,

> The highest virtue, mother of them all,

was the veil of grossness lifted from before his eyes. He had set out upon the quest in a spirit of self-elation. He had come off the victor in the tournament of the day before, and started upon the search with the pride of his victory lifting up his soul:

> And I was lifted up in heart, and thought
> Of all my late shown prowess in the lists;
> How my strong lance had beaten down the knights,
> Many and famous names.

With his heart full of pride, he went forth on the quest; but fruitlessly, for his vice had blinded him:

> Thereafter, the dark warning of our King,
> That most of us would follow wandering fires,

Came like a driving gloom athwart my mind.
Then every evil word I had spoken once,
And every evil thought I had thought of old,
And every evil deed I ever did,
Awoke and cried, "This quest is not for thee!"
And lifting up mine eyes I found myself
Alone, and in a land of sand and thorns;
And I was thirsty even unto death;
And I, too, cried, "This quest is not for thee!"

Percivale has become conscious of the barrenness
of his own soul; it is a land of sand and thorns, a
desert land where grows no fruit. Wheresoever he
goes, there does he find an image of the desolation
in his own soul, whatsoever he touches falls into
dust:

But even while I drank the brook and ate
The goodly apples, all these things at once
Fell into dust and I was left alone,
And thirsting, in a land of sand and thorns.

In the midst of his bootless wanderings he comes
across

A holy hermit in a hermitage,
To whom I told my phantoms, and he said:
"O son, thou hast not true humility,
The highest virtue, mother of them all;
For when the Lord of all things made Himself
Naked of glory for His mortal change,

'Take thou my robe,' she said, 'for all is thine.'
And all her form shone forth with sudden light.
So that the angels were amazed and she
Followed Him down, and like a flying star
Led on the gray-haired wisdom of the East;
But her thou hast not known: for what is this
Thou thoughtest of thy prowess and thy sins?
Thou hast not lost thyself to save thyself
As Galahad."

Humility is the all essential virtue to spiritual
insight. Not until Percivale has purged his soul of
the grossness of pride may he see the Holy Grail.
But Galahad saw from the beginning. With him
the eyes of the soul have never been blinded by sin,
and the Holy Grail, the spiritual vessel, was ever
present to him:

. . . And in the strength of this I rode,
Shattering all evil customs everywhere,
And passed through pagan realms and made them mine,
And clashed with pagan hordes and bore them down,
And broke through all, and in the strength of this
Come victor.

In the presence of Sir Percivale he mystically
passes into the higher life. At the same moment the
Sacred Vessel becomes visible to Percivale himself:

. . . And thrice above him all the heavens
Opened and blazed with thunder, such as seemed
Shouting of all the sons of God: and first
At once I saw him far on the great sea
In silver shining armor starry clear,
And o'er his head the Holy Vessel hung,
Clothed in white samite or a luminous cloud,
And with exceeding swiftness ran the boat,

. . . .

And o'er his head the Holy Vessel hung,
Redder than any rose, a joy to me,
For now I knew the veil had been withdrawn.

This glimpse of the Holy Vessel sets Percivale's soul aflame with an unquenchable desire for the things of the spiritual world, and abandoning the haunts of men he passes into the silent life.

And so with the other knights who undertake the quest of the Holy Grail. In proportion to their spirituality do they enjoy the sacred vision.

Sir Lancelot, who had undertaken the sacred quest in the hope of ridding himself of his great sin, gets the merest glimpse of the Holy Vessel veiled. He recounts to the King:

. . . But in me lived a sin
So strange, of such a kind, that all of pure,

Noble and knightly in me twined and clung
Round that one sin, until the wholesome flower
And poisonous grew together, each as each,
Not to be plucked asunder; and when thy knights
Sware, I sware with them only in the hope
That could I touch or see the Holy Grail
They might be plucked asunder.

The madness of his sin seizes upon him at the
very outset, the rage of the remorseful struggle
between his better and his lower self. Unlike Tristram, Lancelot never abandons himself to the lusts
of the flesh nor accepts the doctrine of free-love as
the gospel of his conduct. He clings to his sin, it
is true, with affection—and this is the radical vice
of his tentative efforts at repentance—but he sees
the wrong, deplores it bitterly, and strives in a way
to battle against it. Yet he lacks the entire will to
eradicate it, and therefore the ignominious failure
of his quest, whose achievement is granted only to
the pure in heart. His great sin drains him of even
his wonted prowess, and he falls before the lances of
lesser knights in his wanderings:

There was I beaten down by little men,
Mean knights, to whom the moving of my sword
And shadow of my spear had been enow
To scare them from me once.

He comes at length, after drifting seven days and
nights upon the sea in a little boat, to the enchanted
castle of Carbonek:

> A castle like a rock upon a rock,
> With chasm-like portals open to the sea
> And steps that met the breaker.

Two great beasts bar the entrance. They will
tear to pieces him who doubts, but the man of
faith—and such is Lancelot, though a sinner—is
suffered to enter. None may pass into the spiritual
house, wherein the Holy Grail abides, save he who
is panoplied in the armor of faith. Had Tristram
or Gawain essayed, either would have been torn
piecemeal by the two lions. Lancelot, on entering,
hears a sweet voice singing in the topmost tower to
the eastward:

> . . . Up I climbed a thousand steps
> With pain; as in a dream I seemed to climb
> Forever: at the last I reached a door;
> A light was in the crannies, and I heard,
> "Glory and joy and honor to our Lord
> And to the Holy Vessel of the Grail."
> Then in my madness I essayed the door;
> It gave; and thro' a stormy glare, a heat
> As from a seven-times heated furnace, I,

Blasted and burnt, and blinded as I was,
With such a fierceness that I swooned away—
O, yet methought I saw the Holy Grail,
All pall'd in crimson samite, and around
Great angels, awful shapes, and wings and eyes.
And but for all my madness and my sin,
And then my swooning, I had sworn I saw
That which I saw; but what I saw was veil'd
And cover'd; and this quest was not for me.

Impure of heart, Lancelot would have achieved
the quest by violence, but is smitten down, burned
and blasted for his rashness. Yet, insomuch as he
still aspires to higher things, even in the slough of
his sin, he is vouchsafed a glimpse of the Holy
Vessel, but veiled and covered, a prevenient grace to
move him to that life of penance which, in the old
Romance, he afterward followed with ardor and
wholesome sincerity.[8]

When Arthur reproaches his knights with having
sworn hastily and rashly to undertake the quest of
the Holy Grail, inasmuch as they were not all Galahads nor Percivales, and therefore not destined to
the higher life, he tells them that he himself would
not have sworn the vow had he been present when
the Holy Grail flashed upon the vision of the as-
sembled Order of the Round Table; for it behooves

the King to remain at the plow, like the hind to
whom is given his allotted space of land, and who
may not desert his task until his work be done:

> . . . But being done,
> Let visions of the night or of the day
> Come, as they will; and many a time they come,
> Until this earth he walks on seems not earth,
> This light that strikes his eyeball is not light,
> This air that smites his forehead is not air,
> But vision—yea, his very hand and foot—
> In moments when he feels he cannot die,
> And knows himself no vision to himself,
> Nor the high God a vision, nor that One
> Who rose again.

This is the King's—the spiritual man's—asser-
tion of the eternal truth and reality of the spiritual
life as against the evanescent contingencies of temporal things.   At the same time, it is the declara-
tion of the duty of the spiritual man, excepting
Galahads and Percivales, who are especially called,
to fulfill his appointed task in the round of years
allotted to him, and to await, in patience, release
from the bonds of time.   True life is in the con-
summation of the Divine presence by faith in Him
who rose again; there, the substance of the spiritual life, and its last fruition.

Gawain not only has not seen but scoffs at the vision:

> "By mine eyes and by mine ears I swear,
> I will be deafer than the blue-eyed cat,
> And thrice as blind as any noon-day owl
> To holy virgins in their ecstasies
> Henceforward."
>   "Deafer," said the blameless king,
> "Gawain, and blinder unto holy things,
> Hope not to make thyself by idle vows,
> Being too blind to have desire to see."

PELLEAS AND ETTARRE

THIS is the same Gawain who swore to aid Sir Pelleas in winning the love of the cruel Ettarre. Sir Pelleas's soul is aflame with the ideal of knighthood and love. He says to Arthur:

> Make me thy knight, because I know, Sir King,
> All that belongs to knighthood, and I love.

At the court of Arthur he seeks the realization of his fine ideal. The perfect image of true love and the chivalrous life burns in his soul, and he but seeks their realization in the offices of the Round

Table.   The Queen, in his youthful eyes, is the fair
model of his lady love, whom he is yet to find:

> . . . . .   Where?
> O where? I love thee, tho' I know thee not.
> For fair thou art and pure as Guinevere,
> And I will make thee with my spear and sword
> As famous, O my Queen, my Guinevere,
> For I will be thine Arthur when we meet.

On the way to the court he meets Ettarre, also
traveling thither, and pours out upon her the great
abundance of his pent-up love.

> . . . . . .   And Pelleas looked
> Noble among the noble, for he dreamed
> His lady loved him, and he knew himself
> Loved of the King; and him his new-made knight
> Worshipt, whose lightest whisper moved-him more
> Than all the rangèd reasons of the world.

The petulance and cruelty of Ettarre are to him
but the chivalrous trials of love, to be borne cour-
teously and submissively by the knight who would
win the guerdon of his lady's faith.   Ettarre is
only a weaker Vivien.   She hates the King and his
knighthood.   The loyal persistence of Pelleas, in his
service to win her love, enrages her.   She mocks him
and rails at him, thrice thrusting him out of door,

bound and humiliated, but he still believes that she
is only testing his knightly loyalty. It is only when
he finds himself betrayed by Gawain that he awakens to the hideous reality of her falseness and wantonness. When he discovers the false Ettarre and
her brutish crew slumbering after their red-revel
in their golden-peaked pavilions, and Gawain a
traitor in the midst of them, the very framework
of his being is shattered, and he bursts out in a
storm of agonized reproach:

. . . . O towers so strong,
Huge, solid, would that even while I gaze,
The crack of earthquake shivering to your base
Split you, and hell burst up your harlot roofs
Bellowing, and charred you thro' and thro' within,
Black as the harlot's heart, hollow as a skull!

Frenzied and maddened, he rushes from the polluting sight, and in his headlong precipitancy
meets Lancelot,
. . . . . Riding airily,
Warm with a gracious parting from the Queen,

    .   .   .   •   .   .   .

. . . . On whom the boy
Across the silent-seeded meadow-grass
Borne, clashed: And Lancelot, saying, "What name
    hast thou
That ridest here so blindly and so hard?"

"No name, no name," he shouted; " a scourge am I
To lash the treasons of the Table Round."
"Yea, but thy name?" "I have many names," he cried,
"I am wrath and shame and hate and evil fame,
And like a poisonous wind I pass to blast
And blaze the crime of Lancelot and the Queen."

Pelleas, in his madness, is but the dire image of
Lancelot's sin. He typifies the sensual man blown
about by the fury of his own passions, a poisonous
wind, to blast and kill. Passion is a fury, and
drives its victims forever on the wings of eternal
blasts, a picture presented to us by Dante in that
circle of the Inferno where Francesca and Paolo
bemoan their sin, where

. . . . . The stormy blast of hell
With restless fury drives the spirits on,
Whirled round and dashed amain with sore annoy.

Pelleas, after his overthrow by Lancelot, breaks
headlong into the hall in the presence of Guinevere and her knight and dames, and the Queen offers
consolation to the stricken youth, saying:

"Or hast thou other griefs? If I, the Queen,
May help them, loose thy tongue, and let me know."

But Pelleas lifted up an eye so fierce
She quailed, and he, hissing "I have no sword,"
Sprang from the door into the dark.   The Queen
Looked hard upon her lover, he on her,
And each foresaw the dolorous day to be;
And all talk died, as in a grove all song
Beneath the shadow of some bird of prey;
Then a long silence came upon the hall,
And Modred thought, "The time is hard at hand."

Until now the sin of Lancelot and the Queen had been working in the veins, subtly and silently poisoning and sowing the seed of the wrath to come. In the Idyll of *Pelleas and Ettarre* it at last bursts forth in fury, and the foul ensample drawn from noble names makes pollution throughout the land. Modred, the traitor, has been waiting the fatal hour when he might strike, in the assurance that the sin of the flesh has undermined the fair structure of the Round Table. In *Geraint and Enid* the shadow of the great sin had fallen ominously but not fatally; in *Balin and Balan* it leads to violence, and disaster in the slaughter of the two brothers; in *Pelleas and Ettarre* it blasts the great ideal of the Round Table and rolls its black wave to the foot of the throne itself; in *The Last Tournament* its murky waters rise to engulf all.

THE LAST TOURNAMENT

WHEN Arthur was made one with Guinevere by Dubric, the high priest, the world was white with May ; it was the springtime, the season of the blossom and the promise of the fullness of the time to come. The chronological setting of *The Last Tournament* is in the season of the yellowing woods and the falling leaf, and we find King Arthur fighting his last great battle in the west,

> . . . That day when the great light of heaven
> Burn'd at his lowest in the rolling year.

This temporal framework is the external symbolism of the seasons of human life, the spiritual passage through the avenues of time from birth to death:

> From the great deep to the great deep he goes.

It is also the symbol of the moral growth and then the decadence of the Round Table through the corrupting influence of the Queen's great sin. The sad presage of dying nature in Autumn's melancholy englooms the events of the last tournament given by Arthur, the "Tournament of the Dead Innocence."

The prize is a carcanet of rubies found about the neck of a maiden babe rescued by Arthur and Lancelot from an eagle's nest. The babe is given to Guinevere to rear, but dies, and the Queen, delivering the necklace to the King, says:

Take thou the jewels of this dead innocence,
And make them, an thou wilt, a tourney-prize.

.   .   .   .

Perchance—who knows?—the purest of thy knights
May win them for the purest of my maids

Guinevere's words are interpreted into a broad irony by Tristram's winning the carcanet of rubies, Tristram, the lover of Isolt, the wife of King Mark, and the faithless husband of Isolt of Brittany. Dagonet, the King's jester, makes fine raillery over the untoward outcome of the Tournament of the Dead Innocence, in his reply to the caviling Tristram:

But Dagonet, with one foot poised in his hand,
"Friend, did ye mark that fountain yesterday
Made to run wine? But this had run itself
All out like a long life to a sour end;

And them that round it sate with golden cups
To hand the wine to whosoever came—
The twelve small damosels white as Innocence,
In honor of poor Innocence the babe,
Who left the gems which Innocence the Queen
Lent to the King, and Innocence the King
Gave for a prize—and one of those white slips
Handed her cup, and piped, the pretty one,
' Drink, drink, Sir Fool,' and thereupon I drank,
Spat—pish—the cup was gold, the draught was mud."

Yes, it is the last tournament, the tournament of
the dead innocence of Guinevere, fittingly won by
Tristram, the free-lover. The golden cup of
Arthur's table now holds but the muddy lees of
Lancelot's and her sin. Tristram now openly pro-
claims the doctrine of lust:

Free love—free field—we love but while we may ;
The woods are hushed, their music is no more ;
The leaf is dead, the yearning past away :
New leaf, new life, the days of frost are o'er ;
New life, new love, to suit the newer day :
New loves are sweet as those that went before ;
Free love—free field—we love but while we may.

Tristram expostulates with Dagonet, the King's
jester, for not dancing to the music of his song.

And while he twanged, little Dagonet stood
Quiet as any water-sodden log
Stayed in the wandering warble of a brook.

Dagonet declares that there is no music in Tristram's harping. It is nothing but discord, says the jester, because it breaks the heavenly harmony of the Round Table. " In heaven," says Dagonet, " there is a star we call the harp of Arthur."

. . . "Do ye see it?   Do ye see the star?"
"Nay, fool," said Tristram, "not in open day."
And Dagonet, " Nay nor will ; I see it and hear.
It makes a silent music up in heaven,
And I, and Arthur, and the angels hear,
And then we skip."   " Lo, fool," he said, " ye talk
Fool's treason ; is the King thy brother fool?"
Then little Dagonet clapped his hands and shrilled,
" Ay, ay, my brother fool, the king of fools."

Arthur's music is the soul's harmony to which is built the city of God, up in heaven, therefore. The beautiful house which the soul has builded up to the music of truth and goodness falls into ruin under the weight of sin. Tristram cannot hear Arthur's music, for he has sinned viciously and wantonly ; the ears of his soul are clogged with the lusts of the flesh. Discord has silenced the music of

the spiritual house; the flesh has rebelled against
the sovereignty of the soul, and Arthur's work is
thus undone.   Lancelot and the Queen are the first
to break that bond.   Then follows the sin of Tristram and Isolt.

Then others, following these my mightiest knights,
And drawing foul ensample from fair names,
Sinned also.

GUINEVERE

THE passions, let loose from the bridle of restraint, finally leap beyond all curb.   One defection
succeeds another; treachery, treason, and war
quickly follow; peace dies and strife is again born.
The Queen flees and seeks refuge in the monastery
of Almesbury.

.   .   .   .   .   Her cause of flight
Sir Modred; he that like a subtle beast
Lay couchant with his eyes upon the throne,
Ready to spring, waiting a chance.

Treason, making its way through the breach
wrought by passion, plays its sinister part.   Passion and malice alike combine against the stricken
soul.

To Almesbury the great King comes to forgive

Guinevere, but to reproach her as well with his
great undoing:

> . . . Prone from off her seat she fell,
> And groveled with her face against the floor;
> There, with her milkwhite arms and shadowy hair,
> She made her face a darkness from the King.
>
> .   .   .   .
>
> "Lo, I forgive thee as eternal God
> Forgives; do thou for thine own soul the rest."

Arthur passes from her presence in the hope that

> Hereafter, in that world where all are pure,
> We two may meet before high God, and thou
> Wilt spring to me and claim me thine, and know
> I am thine husband—not a smaller soul,
> Nor Lancelot, nor another.

THE PASSING OF ARTHUR

THE smoldering fires of treason have now broken
out in open rebellion, and from Almesbury the King
goes to fight that last great fight before he passes.[10]
Arthur is forewarned of his coming departure by
the ghost of Gawain, who, blown

> Along a wandering wind and past his ear
> Went shrilling, "Hollow, hollow, all delight!

Hail, King, to-morrow thou shalt pass away;
Farewell ! There is an isle of rest for thee,
And I am blown along a wandering wind,
And hollow, hollow, all delight."

This is Gawain, light of love and faithless to his friend, the mocker of holy virgins in their ecstasies, and now forever blown about upon a wandering wind, and, like Dante's Francesca, bewailing that irrevocable past, once reveled in as the very substance of life, now found empty, the vanity of the world. But to Arthur, the spiritual man, who has stood firm amidst the shocks of conflict and the onslaughts of temptation, he promises rest and peace, and then passes on with his perpetual wail of sorrow.

Then follows the great battle in the west with its Homeric proportions.

And there, that day, when the great light of heaven
Burned at his lowest in the rolling year,
On the waste sand by the waste sea they closed.
   .   .   .   .

. . . But when the dolorous day
Grew drearier, toward twilight falling, came
A bitter wind, clear from the North, and blew
The mist aside, and with that wind the tide
Rose, and the pale King glanced across the field

Of battle; but no man was moving there,
Nor any cry of Christian heard thereon,
Nor yet of heathen, only the wan wave
Brake in among dead faces, to and fro
Swaying the helpless hands, and up and down
Tumbling the hollow helmets of the fallen,
And shivered brands that once had fought with **Rome;**
And rolling far along the gloomy shores
The voice of days of old and days to be.

The work of destruction had been done; desolation and sorrow and silence had fallen upon the soul, and Arthur, sorely wounded, lay smitten,

And all his greaves and cuisses dashed with drops
Of onset, and the light and lustrous curls—
That made his forehead like a rising sun
High from the dais-throne—were parched with dust,
Or, clotted into points and hanging loose,
Mixed with the knightly growth that fringed his lips.
So, like a shattered column, lay the King.

Arthur and Bedivere remain alone upon the field, and Bedivere, in the full puissance of faith, hails him King even in that last extremity:

. . . . . . My King,
King everywhere; and so the dead have **kings,**
There also will I worship thee as King.

Modred, the traitor, suddenly appears near them,
and Bedivere points him out to the stricken King:

  . . . . . He that brought
The heathen back among us yonder stands,
Modred, unharmed, the traitor of thine house.
Then spake the King: "My house has been my doom,
But call not thou this traitor of my house,
Who hath but dwelt beneath one roof with me.
My house are rather those who sware my vows,
Yea, even while they brake them, owned me King.
And well for thee, saying, in my dark hour,
When all the purport of my throne hath failed,
That, quick or dead, thou holdest me for King;
King am I, whatsoever be their cry."

Through Modred's treason the heathen have
been brought back; internal discord has opened
the doors to the foes without; the lower man,
through sin, has betrayed the peace and unity of
the soul, whose integrity, now shattered, lies ex-
posed to the attacks of all malignants. Bedivere
still owns Arthur King, and reiterates his fidelity
and allegiance. The spiritual man, in the midst of
all afflictions, rebelled against and betrayed, still
asserts his authority, and, rising up in the dignity
of his right, cries out:

King am I, whatsoever be their cry.

Those are of his household who swear his vows,
and even in the breaking of them, spite of their
perfidy, must own him King, as did Gawain, in the
vision, when he addressed Arthur, " Hail, King!"
Sorely wounded, Arthur commands Sir Bedivere to
throw his brand Excalibur into the lake, and then
report to him what happens.   After being twice
faithless, through temptation of the riches of the
hilt, Bedivere flings Excalibur into the mere, and
reports to Arthur:

> Then with both hands I flung him, wheeling him,
> But when I looked again, behold, an arm
> Clothed in white samite, mystic, wonderful,
> That caught him by the hilt and brandished him
> Three times, and drew him under in the mere.

The soul's spiritual weapon, by which it had
smitten its enemies in the battle of life, is returned
to Religion, the Lady of the Lake; for there is no
longer need of it on the journey to the Isles of
Rest, where is no warfare, but peace and ease.
Arthur is borne by Bedivere to the shore, where
lies a black barge, whose

. . . Decks were dense with stately forms,
Black-stoled, black-hooded, like a dream—by these
Three queens with crowns of gold.

These are the three queens who should help
Arthur at his need; the three theological virtues,
now come to the assistance of the faithful soul
passing to the eternity beyond, there to crown it.
Bedivere, at the King's command, places him on
the barge, whence Arthur addresses him before
departing:

The old order changeth, yielding place to new,
And God fulfills Himself in many ways,
Lest one good custom should corrupt the world.

The time has come when the pearl is to be sun-
dered from the shell, when the soul passes from
the old order, life in the flesh, to the new order
beyond space and time. Slowly moves the sable
barge from the shore, and, with its wailing figures,
vanishes beyond the horizon, and Bedivere stands
gazing after it,

Straining his eyes beneath an arch of hand.

He has passed; the spiritual fight is over.

And the new sun rose, bringing the new year.

NOTES

1. *Geoffrey's or Malory's [Malleor's] book;* the source of the Arthurian legends which Tennyson followed. The Geoffrey alluded to is Geoffrey of Monmouth, probably a Benedictine monk of Monmouth, author of the *Historia Regum Britanniæ* (History of the Kings of Britain), written in Latin. He lived in the twelfth century and was consecrated Bishop of St. Asaph in 1152, and died some two years after. His history professes to be derived from an ancient Cymric chronicle brought from Brittany by Walter, Archdeacon of Oxford. Some critics allege that Geoffrey's *Historia* was compiled from the Latin Nennius (a reputed author of the *Historia Britonum*, about the ninth century) and a book of Breton legends now lost. The story of King Arthur, who is supposed to have reigned in the sixth century, was made current generally by Geoffrey's book. "The publication of this book," says the Dictionary of National Biography, "marks an epoch in the literary history of Europe; in less than fifty years the Arthurian and Round Table romances based on it were naturalized in Germany and Italy as well as in France and England."

It is from Malory's book *Morte Darthur* that Tennyson immediately drew the materials and the story of the *Idylls of the King.* Sir Thomas Malory lived in the fifteenth century, and, according to his own words, was a knight. Some have inferred that he was also a priest, from his statement that he was "a servant of Jesu both day and night"; but the illation is by no means flawless, as a layman in that age of outspoken piety might as readily have so characterized himself. Malory tells us that he finished the book in the ninth year of Edward IV's reign, or in 1470. Fifteen years afterwards, in 1485, it was published by Caxton, the first English printer. Tennyson follows Malory's story in its main narrative and in its ethical lines, while he smoothes away its inconsistencies and its confusions and refines with a modern touch its rugged contour.

Sir Edward Strachy, in his introduction to the Globe editions of *Morte Darthur* (Macmillan & Co.), summarizes the character of Malory's book as follows: "The plan of the book is properly epic. While the glory of Arthur, as the head of the kingdoms no less than of the chivalry of Christendom, is only in its early dawn, Merlin warns him that the seeds of death will spring up in all this fair promise through the sin of himself and of his Queen. Still the fame and the honor of the King and his knights of the Round Table open continually into new and brighter forms, which seem above the reach of any adverse fate, till the coming of the Sancgrael, into the quest of which all the knights enter with that self-reliance which had become them so well in the field of worldly chivalry, but which would be of no avail now. They are now to be tried by other tests than those by which they had been proved 'earthly knights and lovers,' tests which even Launcelot, Ector de Maris, Gawain, and the other chiefest of the fellowship could not stand. The quest is achieved by the holy knights alone; two depart from this life to a higher, while Sir Bors, not quite spotless, yet forgiven and sanctified, the link between the earthly and the spiritual worlds, returns to aid in restoring the glory of the feasts and tournaments at Camelot and Westminster. But the curse is at work: the severance between good and evil which had been declared through the Sancgrael cannot be closed again; and the tragic end comes on, in spite of the efforts—touching from their very weakness—of Arthur and Launcelot to avert the woe, the one by vainly trying to resist temptation, the other by refusing to believe evil of his wife and his dearest friend. The black clouds open for a moment as the sun goes down, and we see Arthur in the barge which bears him to the Holy Isle; Guinevere, the nun of Almesbury, living in fasting, prayers, and alms-deeds; and Launcelot with his fellowship, once knights, now hermit-priests, 'doing bodily all manner of service.' "

It will be seen from the above outline how closely Tennyson adheres in its broad lines to the fashion of his original. But it must not be imagined that the author of the *Idylls of the King* sought merely to versify Malory's story. While faithful to the inspiration of his source, the poet not only remodeled and refined Malory's crude material, but has recreated the story without losing its profound ethical value, and adapted it with consummate artistic skill to modern appreciation without sacrificing its mediæval spirit. His Arthur, "the faultless King, that passionate perfection," is not altogether Malory's hero, who is by no means blameless, and whose sin, as well as Guinevere's and Lancelot's, concurs in bringing about the destruction of the Round Table. Tennyson gives us a perfect king and gentleman, whose character is a sublimation of Malory's ancient emperor, and yet in general contour reflects, idealized, it is true, the heroic features of the legendary son of Uther Pendragon. As he has idealized Arthur without losing the mediæval character of the royal hero, so has he treated in general the "old imperfect tale, new-old," on idealized lines, lifting it out of its ruder historic-legendary setting and adapting it to his purpose of " shadowing sense at war with soul," that it might point a moral to his own generation. "A truth looks freshest in the fashion of the day" was Everard Hall's (Tennyson's) reason for not publishing his epic of King Arthur. But a riper judgment led the poet to enshrine that truth in the old legend made anew by his genius.

2. The episode of Arthur's "desire to be joined with Guinevere" strikes a profound note of Tennyson's muse, which sounds, in an especial way, throughout the Idylls and in his greater poems. An insistent doctrine in his philosophy of life is the fundamental need of the purity and permanency of the family in order to insure human growth and progress. In pure and stable wedded love is

at once the hope and perfection of man's social life No poet sings the promise or fulfillment of wedded passion with a purer and clearer note. To break the bond of marital affection and faith is to destroy human society at its foundation, and it is this dire sin in Guinevere which brings about the ruin of Arthur's kingdom. It is only in wedded union with the Queen that the King

> Has power on this dark land to lighten it,
> And power on this dead world to make it live.

Tennyson's lofty ideal of the married state may be gathered from the severe probation which Arthur imposes upon his knights before they may attain the goal of their desire:

> I made them lay their hands in mine and swear
> To reverence the King as if he were
> Their conscience, and their conscience as their King,
> To break the heathen and uphold the Christ,
> To ride abroad redressing human wrongs,
> To speak no slander, no, nor listen to it,
> To honor their own word as if their God's,
> To lead sweet lives in purest chastity,
> To love one maiden only, cleave to her,
> And worship her by years of noble deeds,
> Until they won her.

In *The Two Voices*, in which the problem is suicide as it addresses itself to the modern skeptic under the burden of life's ills, we find the gloom of doubt and despair utterly dispelled in the contemplation of the serene unity of the family in the father, the mother, and the child:

> These three made unity so sweet,
> My frozen heart began to beat,
> Remembering its ancient heat.

> I blest them, and they wandered on;
> I spoke, but answer came there none:
> The dull and bitter voice was gone.

In *The Princess*, whose theme is the very modern question of the proper sphere of woman, the solution comes with no uncertain voice that in the family life alone, as wife and mother, is to be found her true place, her real equality, and the divinely ordained complement of her nature:

> The woman's cause is man's: they rise or sink
> Together, dwarf'd or godlike, bond or free.
>
> .   .   .   .
>
> For woman is not undeveloped man,
> But diverse: could we make her as the man,
> Sweet Love were slain; his dearest bond is this,
> Not like to like, but like in difference.
> Yet in the long years liker must they grow;
> The man be more of woman, she of man;
> He gain in sweetness and in moral height,
> Nor lose the wrestling thews that throw the world;
> She mental breadth, nor fail in childward care,
> Nor lose the childlike in the larger mind;
> Till at the last she set herself to man,
> Like perfect music unto noble words.

In Memoriam, whose song rises by degrees from the wail of the threnody through the swelling note of Hope into the triumphant acclaim of Faith and Love, concludes with a wedding song, the mystery of death answered and solved by the mystery of life, whose fountains lie in the unity and purity of the family. Here issues the stream of humanity to that

> .   .   .   One far-off divine event
> To which the whole creation moves.

3. The time-element in the Idylls develops with their ethical movement and symbolizes it. It is in the earlier spring that Lancelot goes to the court of Leodogran to escort Guinevere to King Arthur:

> And Lancelot past away among the flowers
> (For then was latter April) and returned
> Among the flowers, in May, with Guinevere.

It is when "the world is white with May " that Dubric, the
high priest, marries Arthur and Guinevere. It was "past the
time of Easterday" when Gareth set forth for the mystic city of
Camelot. It is just after Whitsuntide that Geraint goes on the
quest which results in his marriage with Enid. In the first
three Idylls, *The Coming of Arthur*, *Gareth and Lynette*, and *The
Marriage of Geraint*, we see the springtime of the Round Table,
when all is fresh and fair, without taint or flaw amongst Arthur's
knighthood. Beginning with *Geraint and Enid*, the summer sets
in, and continuous throughout the action (in the order here enu-
merated) of *Balin and Balan*, *Merlin and Vivien*, *Lancelot and
Elaine*, *The Holy Grail*, and comes to its close in *Pelleas and
Ettarre*. An ever-deepening note of menace to Arthur's work
swells with the advancing summertide, as the poison of Guinevere's sin spreads throughout the Order of the Round Table,
until it moans through the "yellowing woods," the hour of the
"withered leaf," the season of the Last Tournament.

> All in a death-dumb autumn dripping gloom.

Guinevere and *The Passing of Arthur* close the symbolic time-
cycle in the deep winter. Beyond the convent walls, where the
guilty Queen harbors,

> The white mist, like a face-cloth to the face,
> Clung to the dead earth, and the land was still.

Arthur's last great battle is in midwinter in the barren land
of Lyonesse:

> There the pursuer could pursue no more,
> And he that fled no further fly the King;
> And there, that day when the great light of heaven
> Burned at his lowest in the rolling year,
> On the waste sand by the waste sea they closed.

Arthur, "a naked babe," is cast at the feet of Merlin by the
ninth wave of the great deep on the "night of the new year." He

passes now at the close of the old year out into the great deep again, according to Merlin's words,

From the great deep to the great deep he goes.

4. In the early Church during the Roman persecutions there grew up an exigent custom of carefully guarding the graver mysteries of the Faith from the heathen, and also from neophytes who were still under instruction. Symbols of the more sacred doctrines and rites were often used between Christians, which to them conveyed a hidden meaning, but were unintelligible to the heathen about them. Amongst these symbols the most conspicuous was the Greek word for fish, Ἰχθύς, to indicate Christ, as the letters composing this word made the initials of the sentence: Ἰησοῦς χριστὸς θεοῦ υἱος σωτήρ, Jesus Christ, Son of God, Saviour. The Christian inscription discovered at Autun, France, in 1839, has reference to Christ in the Holy Eucharist under the symbol of the sacred fish: "Take the food sweet as honey of the Savior of the holy ones, eat and drink holding the fish in the hands." It was the custom in the primitive Church to receive the sacred Species first in the hands, then in the mouth, of the communicant. Ecclesiastical historians call this practice of concealing the mysteries from the heathen and neophytes, Disciplina Arcani, The Discipline of the Secret.

5. Tennyson, in *Balin and Balan*, depicts the household of King Pellam as an instance of religious decadence in contrast with the pure and active piety of Arthur's court. Pellam's castle is filled with spurious relics, which absorb the false devotion of the decrepit King, who makes claim to be the descendant of Joseph of Arimathea. The spear which Balin seizes in Pellam's chapel, when pursued by the latter's followers, is not the true spear which pierced Christ's side; its point is painted red to simulate the blood which ever moistens the sanctified tip of the true weapon. Malory, however, draws no such contrast between Pellam's and Arthur's courts, and speaks of the spear with which Balin wounds King

Pellam as the authentic lance. When Balin sacrilegiously uses
the sacred glaive, the castle falls in ruins about him and King
Pellam. Cf. *Morte Darthur*, Book II., Chaps. xiv., xv.

6. The element of pure malice, in the person of Vivien, appears
for the first time in *Balin and Balan*. Vivien is the incarnation of
envy and hate. She describes herself in the succeeding Idyll as
one "born from death" and "sown upon the wind." Her song in
Balin and Balan chimes significantly with Tristram's free-love
rhymes in *The Last Tournament*. In her words sounds the dread
menace of the undoing of the Round Table. She sings the
renaissance of the ancient paganism, the old sun-worship of the
land, and bitterly scoffs at the Christian teachings of self-repres-
sion and chastity:

> Old priest, who mumbles worship in your quire,
> Old monk and nun, ye scorn the world's desire,
> Yet in your frosty cells ye feel the fire!
> The fire of heaven is not the flame of hell.

She loathes Arthur and his Round Table, whose ideal is the
direct opposite of the sensual paganism she proclaims. She
would destroy him and his knighthood and bring back the old
sun-worship, which Christianity has supplanted in the land:

> Then turning to her squire, "This fire of heaven,
> This old sun-worship, boy, will rise again,
> And beat the cross to earth, and break the King
> And all his Table."

7. "The hart with golden horns," whose pursuit by the
Knights of the Round Table is narrated by Merlin, appears to be
glory or fame. The second story told by Merlin, of

> A maid so smooth, so white, so wonderful,
> They said a light came from her when she moved,

would seem to convey the symbol of the image of beauty, whose
"isle-nurtured eyes" waged such unwilling though successful

war. The "little glassy-headed, hairless man" to whom the
wall,

> That sunders ghosts and shadow-casting men,
> Became a crystal, and he saw them thro' it,
> And heard their voices talk behind the wall,
> And learnt their elemental secrets, powers,
> And forces,

I take to be wisdom. He alone knows the charm to overcome
the power of beauty and hold it bound.

8. In the concluding lines of Lancelot and Elaine, Tennyson
gives us a hint of Sir Lancelot's end:

> So groaned Sir Lancelot in remorseful pain,
> Not knowing he should die a holy man.

It would not have been consistent with the scope and purpose
of the *Idylls of the King* to pursue the career of Sir Lancelot
to the end. The passing of King Arthur is clearly the fit conclu-
sion. In Malory's story, Sir Lancelot repents and becomes a
monk, doing penance for his past sins during the last seven years
of his life, and is buried at his castle of Joyous Gard. See *Morte
Darthur*, Book XXI., Chap. ix. *et seq.*

9. The Holy Grail or Sancgrael was the vessel or cup used by
Our Lord and His disciples at the last supper, and afterwards by
Joseph of Arimathea to receive the blood from the wounds of
Christ on the cross. The author of *The High History of the
Holy Grail* (probably the original of the Grail legends of the
Middle Ages) says in his opening words: "Hear ye the history
of the most holy vessel that is called Grail, wherein the precious
blood of the Savior was received on the day that He was put on
rood and crucified in order that He might redeem His people from
the pains of hell." (Translation by Sebastian Evans in The
Temple Classics.) A passage from the Chronicle of Helinand
(about 1220), quoted by Mr. Evans in the epilogue to his translation of *The High History of the Holy Grail*, gives the following

account of the Sancgrael: "At this time a certain marvelous vision
was revealed by an angel to a certain hermit in Britain concerning
St. Joseph, the decurion who deposed from the cross the body of
Our Lord, as well as concerning the paten or dish in the which
Our Lord supped with His disciples, whereof the history was
written out by the said hermit and is called 'Of the Grail' (*de
Gradali*). Now a platter, broad and somewhat deep, is called
in French *gradalis* or *gradale*, wherein costly meats with their
sauce are wont to be set before rich folk by degrees (*gradatim*),
one morsel after another in divers orders, and in vulgar speech
it is called *graalz*, for that it is grateful and acceptable to him
that eateth therein, as well for that which containeth the victual,
for that haply it is of silver or other precious metal, as for the
contents thereof, to wit, the manifold courses of costly meats."
This cup or grail containing the precious blood was brought,
according to the legend, by Joseph of Arimathea, the aforesaid
decurion, to Glastonbury. When the people of the land fell
into wickedness it was taken up to heaven, to return only when
they shall have once more entered into the ways of holiness.

10. In Arthur's words, just before the great battle in the west,
is expressed the agony of the spiritual man seeing how the evil
of life would seem to trample down the good:

> I found Him in the shining of the stars,
> I marked Him in the flowering of His fields,
> But in His ways with men I find Him not.
> I waged His wars, and now I pass and die.
> O me! for why is all around us here
> As if some lesser god had made the world,
> But had not force to shape it as he would
> Till the High God behold it from beyond,
> And enter it and make it beautiful?
> Or else as if the world were wholly fair,
> But that these eyes of men are dense and dim,
> And have not power to see it as it is:
> Perchance, because we see not to the close;
> For I, being simple, thought to work His will,

And have but stricken with the sword in vain;
And all whereon I leaned in wife and friend
Is traitor to my peace, and all my realm
Reels back into the beast, and is no more.
My God, thou hast forgotten me in my death:
Nay—God, my Christ—I pass, but shall not die.

Notwithstanding the darkness that comes over his soul, his faith rises triumphant in this his hour of agony. His faith is all in Christ, through whom he shall not die. In the closing scene of *The Passing of Arthur*, Tennyson follows Malory's account in spirit and substance. Cf. *Morte Darthur*, Book XXI., Chaps. iv. and v.

THE END